May 2019

oi Kathy,

With love, blessing
and gratitude always

Carol M. H.

MW00932268

HILDA

HEALTH IMBALANCE LEUKEMIA DIAGNOSIS ADVENTURE

CAROL M. H. ROTH

BALBOA.
PRESS
A DIVISION OF HAY HOUSE

Balboa Press books may be ordered through booksellers or by contacting:

Balboa Press
A Division of Hay House
1663 Liberty Drive
Bloomington, IN 47403
www.balboapress.com
1 (877) 407-4847

Print information available on the last page.

ISBN: 978-1-5043-5913-9 (sc)
ISBN: 978-1-5043-5914-6 (hc)
ISBN: 978-1-5043-5931-3 (e)

Library of Congress Control Number: 2016908714

Balboa Press rev. date: 06/08/2016

For Maggie, who taught me that absolutely everything gets better, no matter what.

To Saint Francis and the Roth Labrador retrievers (a.k.a., Katie, Charlie, and Buster), gratitude for the unwavering inspiration and love throughout our Hilda adventure.

CONTENTS

Part III: The Goods

FOREWORD

Who is your "best self"? You know what I am talking about. Think of a time when your soul was singing brightly with positivity; your faith was unfaltering; your heart was full of love and kindness; and you felt strong and confident. Your "best self" could change the world with your smile alone! We've all had that feeling. Perhaps it began with a great day at work, where you made a difference in someone's life. Perhaps you spent the day serving others, and you felt profoundly changed by the people you served. Maybe it was being outside on a spectacular day, enjoying whatever splendor the day had to offer. On these occasions, you felt centered and were facing the direction of your dreams. You were your favorite possible self.

So when was the last time you saw your "best self"? How often do you hang out with him/her? When was the last time you had a really bad day? Perhaps you had car problems, or a check bounced. Maybe you got in a fight with your best friend or snagged a really bad cold. Did your "best self" show up on those days? Does your "best self" only show up on the good days? Do you think you would be your "best self" if you were diagnosed with an incurable disease?

Hilda is a symbolic book about a woman, her two alter egos, and an elephant who are forced to figure out how to cohabitate. One of the alter egos sees possibility and good in all things. The other represents the part of her that isn't always perfect. Then there is a horrific elephant who may or may not have some redeeming qualities, who relentlessly wreaks havoc in the life of "her roommates."

Carol Roth introduces us to Maggie, Carol Margaret, and Hilda. As readers, we can relate to each one of these personas, and as you get to know them, you will learn to love and appreciate each one, just as our author has done.

This is the story of Carol's journey through a chronic and supposedly incurable disease, from diagnosis to the current day. She shares realistic fears and doubts from her "pragmatic self" and winning strategies for positivity and faith from her "best self." Together, they learn to adapt to living life with an elephant they address as Hilda (health imbalance+ leukemia diagnosis=adventure).

I know her story well and have eagerly anticipated the arrival of this book. As a witness to Carol Roth's journey, I can attest to the fact that she has been on a truly wild ride, and she is still standing strong and tall to share the story.

This book was originally written to help Carol heal. Even though she lived through this amazing ride despite all the odds, she didn't go through it unscathed. Sharing her story, including the struggles and the victories, is her way to acknowledge not only that it happened but also that it is over.

Carol refers to this as her "adventure." That's quite a euphemism for a story where she gets to endure a lot of pain and suffering and do a tango with death more than once. That's because this adventure, in her mind, is not about her as much as it is about the uncanny ability to find good, love, and God in everything. For her, this story is about sharing the gifts this experience provided her. Her story of transformation can translate into all of our lives. All of us deal with challenges, illnesses, even tragedies throughout the course of living. How we face them may not always affect the outcome, but it certainly affects our attitudes and ability to deal with what life throws our way. Carol suggests we can look for good, love, and God as we work through our doubts, fears, and challenges. She shows the gifts present in all experiences as we open our hearts to them. She inspires us to love ourselves, even when our warts are flaring. And although we may not choose to invite elephants or other beasts into our lives, we can learn to coexist with them and find the gifts that are hidden in the most unlikely places.

I know you will be inspired by my sister's story, and I am willing to bet that her experience will help you reflect on your own "elephant" gifts as well.

Susan Marie Hohlfelder Ferreri

INTRODUCTION

My given legal name is Carol Margaret Hohlfelder Roth. Most people know me by some combination or derivative of those four names.

I call myself Maggie, a diminutive of Carol Maggie, the name my parents called me in frequent and fond moments of endearment, exasperation, befuddlement, amusement, and memory. When I'm being an adult, heady, not embraced by brevity or clarity, nerdy, or less than everything wonderful, I call myself Carol, or Carol Margaret when I'm especially harsh with myself. The me I love most is Maggie.

I've lived over half a century at this point, and yet deep down inside, I feel and express myself at my best moments as magical, marvelous Maggie, the one who I am when my spirit soars and my soul sings at the phenomenal joy of being alive, free, and me. I celebrate being a wife, mother, grandmother, sister, aunt, friend, and thoroughly beloved creation of the goodness that made me. I get to celebrate my incredible life as one new adventure after another, and how awesome is that?!

Not to say that creating incredible or amazing life adventures is easy, fun, or happy. At many moments, it is ... except when it's not.

Regardless, I love when I get to learn about myself, life, love, and how I can learn to allow my experience to come to me; to accept what each opportunity brings; to gratefully receive the lessons, learnings, and blessings that come to me; and to fully appreciate with awe-inspired thanksgiving every single experience as an immense gift. Gifts of growth, grace, blessing; of awe, wonder, and amazement; all wrapped in the assurance that, no matter what, everything always resolves or at least reconciles into total possibility—these are the gifts of a grateful and graced life. Thank you, God. Thank you, Maggie!

More than fifty years of embracing Maggie, has brought me to a sacred space in the woods on the path, by the water, with just enough light for the step I'm on. My questions become, "What next do I seek to create with my life? Where do I go, and how do I get there?"

My first question is, "How can I share what I've experienced and learned? What are the ways I've been blessed by my life's experience?" I've always wanted to write stories, and my first thoughts go to Maggie's favorite childhood memories on the porch swing with her beloved grandmother, listening to family stories as they moved with the rhythm of their communion. Or perhaps Maggie could share her discovering and her uncovering with music, art, philosophy, religion, literature, theatre, and dance—an amalgamation of years of learning and loving, all with her very subjective and personal tales of "whats" and "how tos."

Then, and of course, the elephant emerges in broad and inescapable form from the insides of my ancient, cluttered writing desk, and it captures and sustains my full attention as the walls of my office bulge and groan with the immensity of her presence. The elephant in my room I call Hilda: health imbalance + leukemia diagnosis=adventure ... Yes, I now acknowledge her with great fondness. Hilda and I were best buddies for almost fifteen years (except when we weren't). I lived with her from at least 1998 until after 2012—and she may have been there and beyond my awareness before that time. She may come visit me again in the future, but as much as we loved each other, neither of us will choose that reunion. Hilda became one of my best friends (some of the time) before she left my life. On one hand, she brought Carol Margaret more grief, pain, blame, anger, guilt, sorrow, shame, frustration, and suffering than I could ever imagine knowing before I met her. On the other hand, she brought Maggie so many gifts and "goods"—grace, inspiration, passion, acceptance, joy, peace, gratitude, and especially God—as well as many other glorious and indescribable blessings. The three of us as a team taught each other how to heal, love, have fun, survive, let go, surrender, master circumstance, and soar.

This book is a story about Carol, Hilda, and Maggie. Nothing in it makes a whole lot of sense, but this story—like my life—has a whole bunch of unfolding, learning, loving, and God. The intention of this book is to share this adventure from my experience with the hope that, in some small, circuitous way, the awareness, the connections, the happenings, the synchronicities I relate through my story make some kind of difference for the reader. May you, dear reader, feel broadened, blessed, or motivated by your engagement in this story we share, the one we get to call life. I get the challenge and adventure of relaying this particular tale, and I hope you'll see in my story your story as well. We're all in it (whatever it is) together! Thank you, God!

So let me begin this story by introducing you to Hilda ...

The idea of an elephant like Hilda taking over the spaces of my life was beyond my understanding. She was uninvited, unwelcome, unexpected, undesired- and like every other "un" in my life, I didn't want her! She'd been shadowing me for an indeterminate period before I was forced to take ownership of her, but I truly believed Hilda belonged elsewhere—in a zoo or with someone who wanted an elephant in the living room (and every other space) of her life. I did not want to be responsible for the enormity of Hilda and the complexity of what she represented for me. I found her overwhelming and felt frustrated and exasperated that I could not produce an abracadabra and make her disappear from my life. She was huge, real, an attachment to me. From the moment we met, we were inseparable.

Hilda chose me when I was in my late thirties, but she was probably stalking me for years before then. When she first arrived to make my acquaintance, she embraced me with such enthusiasm she took my breath away, almost like she was sitting on my chest (and every other part of me). I was almost nonfunctional at her onslaught. I had not asked to have this creature thrust upon me. She intended to move in with me and take over my life. My cry was a resounding and vehement, *No! No*, I would not allow her to orchestrate my beings, goings, and doings. I would *not* be victimized or controlled by this elephant! I was in charge of how I operated my life, not this humongous animal I didn't even know or like. I felt angry, frustrated, and powerless—almost like I was an imaginary victim-like character in a fun cartoon of *Dumbo*, who suddenly found herself a victim of circumstance in *Elephant Nightmare on Waterstone Way* (the name of the street where I lived at the time).

Maggie, on the other hand, looked at Hilda in awe and reverence, and then remarked, "Oh God! You think we can handle this! Thank you, God!"

Maggie had it made up that God gave great struggles to people/animals/plants (all creation because Maggie's perspective was unlimited) who were ready to embrace trusting God, choosing faith, courage, love—anything that was wanted and needed to survive, thrive, make a difference, and live a "Halleluiah!" Maggie was kind of weird that way. All she thought about night and day was God and goodness, truth, and love. She had this game she played with life, a game of questions. She told me once that she grew tired of fishing for answers because as soon as she caught one, it would slip out of her hands and vanish into a sea of unknowing. "I can question, and one question turns into another, into another, and I keep learning, loving, and finding myself graced and gifted." When I questioned her further (thinking I might beat her at her own game), she said, "Ultimately every present moment is where God is, and the only questions I feel compelled to ask repeatedly are these three: What can I learn? How can I love? Where are you in this experience, God? I always feel better and grateful by those questions, no matter what!"

I thought about what Maggie said, and it prompted more pondering about what life could be like if I could live the questions with Hilda. It certainly couldn't make the situation any worse. I could allow Hilda to be present in my life because I couldn't figure out how to make her disappear. I could accept who she was, and get to know more about her. (What can I learn?) I could figure out how to serve her and our relationship and how to be responsible in my care of her, me, and Maggie. (How can I love?). Maybe, just maybe, I could learn from her and grow to love her? And maybe, just maybe, I could welcome her, invite God to help me with this situation, and accept her as a gift who could grace my life in an extraordinary (albeit cumbersome, smelly, laborious, expensive, exhausting, and awkward) way. Maybe I could choose a perspective where I could really be grateful for her as a gift from God?

I was suffering in my angst and dismay. Hilda, on the other hand, was secure and steadfast in who she was, although within each household she took residence, she behaved differently. I am told she was often a rather mercurial animal, nonconforming and nondiscriminatory with age, race, gender, or creed. She used to hang out with old people mostly—especially men—but as our world has evolved, she has changed. No longer playing favorites, she likes persons of any age or stage of life. She actually described herself to me as aspiring to be the unpredictable Mary Poppins of her breed ... Maggie remarked how much she loved Julie Andrews, and my thought was, *Really?* (I'm trying to keep the questions coming.)

It is often said that dogs choose their people, and Maggie and I have found that to be true with the puppies we've called family. So I wonder what inspired Hilda to choose me. I could read, study, research, and review all the ideas, recommendations, and advice of doctors, experts, healers, intuitives, previous Hilda owners, and the Internet to learn more about her and why she adopted us to be her family. Hilda had a very gentle, loving, rheumy, and kind manner about her when she first came to our home. There was no room in our home big enough to hide her, so everyone knew about her presence at our house. She wasn't especially charming, but she wasn't particularly annoying either ... just big and daunting, in the way, an impediment and potential obstacle for any road I wanted to traverse.

I didn't know what to do with her, so I spent a very long time attempting to ignore her.

Maggie suggested we ride atop Hilda to places we had only dreamed or maybe never even dreamed of imagining we could go. I reflected upon that vision as I gazed into Hilda's truly droopy eyes and wondered, "Why me, God? Why Hilda?" That's when Maggie told me there are no answers to why questions. Carol Margaret, at her assessing, analytical, judgmental best, suggested we follow her well-documented and thoroughly formulated rules about Hilda: Elephant riding was prohibited because it was a less-than- kind treatment and rather abusive use of Hilda, according to her research.

From that place I picked myself up, came to myself, and realized that Carol Margaret Hohlfelder Roth is not just Carol and Maggie. I am Hilda, as well. *Oh God! Help! Thanks! Wow!* All three of Anne Lamott's prayers to pray all at once; Thanks, Anne Lamott!

The Daze

CHAPTER 1

My First Adventure with Hilda

(a.k.a., Meeting Hilda for the Very First
Time, "Daze" I'll Never Forget)

It was a beautiful morning in May when Hilda made her official entrance into our lives. Maggie and I were driving to my Wednesday, 11:00 a.m. tennis lesson and singing sassy songs at our loudest register when my cell phone rudely interrupted our favorite rendition of our current favorite song. My doctor was the caller, and she asked me to pull my car over to the side of the road. As I did so, my heart pounded as if it could expand enough to burst through the confines of my already constricted body. My clammy hands fused with the phone as I paused to park the car and expel the breath I'd been holding to keep from shaking. That's when she told me that Hilda was with me. We had run test upon test because nothing seemed to add up in any understandable, logical, or statistically accurate manner. She reiterated that these characteristics were typical of Hilda and her eccentrically individual style. She referred me to a specialist who knew everything about elephants and set up a time for me to meet with him the next day.

I politely thanked her for the news and then shared that time prompted me to end our call so I would not be late for my tennis lesson.

At this point she exclaimed, "No way can you play tennis. You're too anemic." At that point, Maggie patted my back comfortingly, and I started (sort of) to get the reality of Hilda.

Numbly and with a ghostlike demeanor, I drove Maggie and myself to the tennis club to cancel my lesson. Maggie gently stroked my arm and continued to pat my back the entire ride. From the rearview mirrors, Hilda perched on my car's trunk, waving her wrinkly trunk. She made her first indentation in the body of my car, and I knew it wouldn't be the last. I did not want to deal with her, so I decided to ignore my mirrors and keep my focus on driving forward. Maybe, just maybe, she'd fall off like a bad dream. I was going to keep on keeping on, forward movement, eyes on the road.

Hilda was not a young elephant. She was rather advanced in age, size, and attitude when she moved in with me. The elephant specialist to whom my doctor referred me told me that Hilda and I had the potential to coexist for a very long time with proper treatment, and because I was younger than most of her owners, I could expect new advances in elephant care in my lifetime. There was also the possibility of a transplant down the road, a fun activity where a family member or a stranger who wanted to be family would bring an elephant truck to give me a lift that would empower the elephant to mobilize and disappear.

So many ideas, choices, and questions. At this point, I didn't fully embrace the elephant as Hilda. Initially, I felt totally over, under, and beyond whelmed. Maggie reminded me to slow down enough to breathe, listen, feel, and pray.

You know, this Hilda character, what I imagined in my tongue-in-cheek/foot-in-mouth experience as an elephant, really emanated from a health imbalance well before any cancer diagnosis. Diagnosing an imbalance as dis-ease (a state of being not in-ease) made me think I had done something wrong to have manifested this state of not right. Specifically, when I received a diagnosis of chronic lymphocytic leukemia, I couldn't accept or believe that I would take on the exact elephant my maternal grandfather's death certificate listed as cause of death. I assumed my elephant was a huge mistake, a misdiagnosis, a fallacious labeling. I was not an old man or a farmer like my grandfather, and this particular elephant wasn't overly evidenced to run in families. The Western medicine textbooks didn't consider me a likely or attractive candidate for Hilda.

I wondered, *Why God?* In my search for answers, the questions became learning experiences, creating adventures I could never have imagined before the gift of CLL/Hilda, and the amazing times we shared before I sent her away, like Mary Poppins on her umbrella in the wind. Like Mary Poppins, Hilda transformed my life through grace, gratitude, love, miracles, and an infinite number of "spoonfuls of sugar."

Reflections on First Daze with Hilda

There are all different kinds of animals/imbalances/dis-eases that may move in with us in the course of our lifetimes. How we treat them and ourselves when they're with us determines whether our times together are blessings or burdens, painful or joyful, healing or toxic. The more we learn about our pets/monsters/visitors, the more we get to know ourselves, our courage, our strengths, and our possibilities.

Hilda was my CLL adventure. Woodpeckers may bring with them symptoms suggestive of chronic migraines, or a possum may represent temporary paralysis. These "animals" may come to visit or take residence temporarily or for a very long while. Some of these animals manifest physically like Hilda, and others are invisible to the world, sometimes even to ourselves; revealing who they are and where they're hiding only when we're ready to fully see them. Only when we persist in uncovering what veils our eyes are we able to accept everything ... no matter what. First things first. We get to see to believe so that we learn to lean into embracing possibility (believing without first needing to see).

How I choose to treat myself and the animals I'm aware of are the discovery adventures. How I respond to the introduction of an elephant or a smelly camel, and how I then adjust to coexistence with my animals, determine my reality and the possibility I can create what serves, loves, and glorifies the highest good for all creation.

I am empowered to witness, accept, and adjust to all animals in my life—if I so choose. None of them are bad, wrong, or to be feared unless I imagine them that way. All experience can be neutral, a gift, and another opportunity to blow apart boxes and labels and make miracles of every kind.

All the animals I've ever lived with have just wanted to be accepted— kind of like people do. I want to accept myself and have others accept me, too. Even more than that, I'd love to love unconditionally and experience that same love from others. The first step in that ardent aspiration is to learn about love. That's where the animals bring me the greatest ability to grow and learn. Love is ever present and all pervading. Every single thing I experience helps me learn more about that love I yearn for so intensely.

Many of the animals in my life depart as soon as I become aware of them and acknowledge their presence. I thank them and ask them to leave, or I may persuade them to stay. Some leave before my request, and others hover in the shadows before they slink away.

Some refuse to listen to me. Other animals come in and out of my life as the unfolding of my living plays in and out. Some I welcome as old friends because I've learned from experience how to treat them. Some depart permanently; some leave and return arbitrarily, intermittently paying me a surprise visit. While some of these animals are always discreetly with me, I'm learning how to love them as the gifts they are through an intentioned way of being that supports what I choose to be and to learn because it seems to me that every animal brings another lesson for my highest good.

My higher self (Maggie) leads me to love whenever I allow her guidance. Whenever I choose to love any animal with which I struggle, I am graced by the awareness that I am part of a whole kingdom of living beings that transcends my perception of what

I experience, an awesome oneness that envelops all that is real and true. When I live there, no matter what, I'm in heaven, no matter what lives with me.

So I choose to love, to see good, and to smile when I can. And when I can't, I allow my perception of my experience (separate, angry, pain-filled, ignorant, judgmental, comparing, interpreting, assuming, bored). I persist in my attempts to detach from my experience until I become successful at witnessing with neutrality my "less than" encounter/tantrum/conversation/rage. I reassure myself (Maggie consoles Carol) that it always gets better and that this moment won't make it into the next one. When the not enough/less than energy passes (and it always does), I forgive myself, pick myself up, and choose to love, to see good, and to smile once again. I stay present in the new moment of now. I let go of self-flagellation for my assumed and negative perception of whatever has passed. I embrace what is before me with the absolute love I am.

The gift of meeting Hilda was learning to look at life in a new way, knowing that together we would create a uniquely new adventure unlike any I'd ever imagined or dreamed. No true idea of how it could unfold and an abundance of choices in response loomed before us. In the time I lived with this particular animal, I can almost certify that I experimented with as many reactions, responses, and "how-to-dos" as I recognized. Ultimately, our safari together yielded life-transforming blessings of grace and love. And honestly, on reflection, we really did have fun along the way.

CHAPTER 2

Doctoring Daze: Learning about Hilda, and Hilda Moves In

So after my initial daze cleared into something I could elevate enough to view as topography, we were introduced and became acquainted with the elephant specialist. Actually, he was simply a certain kind of animal trainer, not officially certified as an elephant expert. He used drugs, chemicals, and medicines to control the animals accompanying the patients he doctored. He was about my age when I first met him. He assured me that we would grow old together.

When I was first referred to my trainer/oncologist, I didn't know what I didn't know and even less than that about Hilda/elephants/ CLL/"my type" of cancer. I surmise that most trainers are more comfortable and secure when they are the in-charge authorities. My trainer was kind and reassuring and carried with him an excellent reputation and documents, diplomas, and certificates on his office walls acclaiming and attesting to that evidence of achievement. In his expert opinion, he told me that we should do chemotherapy regularly to train Hilda, keep her under control, and keep me from succumbing to "elephantitis" (a.k.a., too much elephant). He performed tests and procedures to gauge how much Hilda's presence would impact my physical person. He was absolutely assuring and affirmed his accuracy in everything he told me, and I was naïve enough to embrace and absorb every molecule he muttered as gospel. My response was, "Yes sir. Thank you. I will. Amen."

Our trainer employed a wonderful staff of nurses, friendly, helpful, and caring. His office contained an area that I came to call "the chemo corral," where patients and their animals would sit in recliners in stall-like areas and receive drugs to tame the threatening nature of each patient's animal or animals (some brought more than one, but to my eyes, no animal was as big as Hilda). Patients and their animals were infused and injected with needles, tubing, liquids, pills, shots—all given in various inspired ways—through arms, ports, catheters, legs, bellies, pic lines. All modes of delivery were geared to subdue the animals, poison them into submission, send them running away, or dissolve them into the fairytale animals their higher selves aspired to be, an ethereal reality interesting to suppose in my daydreams.

It was kind of voyeuristic to patient and animal watch from my chosen vantage point in the chemo corral. The chemo corral had a shortage of space. There was always a wait, and oftentimes, those patients and their animals were herded to their spots, remaining there for a very long time. Some were quicker movers than others, but there was always a wait—for space, for drugs, for tests, for results, for everything. Maggie suggested we practice patience and paying attention, so I thought I'd give it a try. It made for marvelous entertainment when I was awake enough to notice how we were all part of the same program. Different animals, different patients, different stories, but we all shared this place, this day, these people who treated us, and our individual stalls in the collective chemo corral.

There was a unique assortment of patients and animals, and I searched to no avail for a twin to Hilda. Alas, the other elephants in the corral bore no resemblance to her. I didn't know whether to be proud, humbled, or irritated—how could I figure her out and confine her if there were none like her in the barn?

When we weren't getting treated in the corral, visiting doctors' offices, or playing "ignore Hilda" games (i.e., pretending there's no elephant in the room), I researched everything I could find about Hilda, and the nature of her beast. One weird and absolute rule I established for myself from the get go: *no way* would I ever purchase elephant books/books about cancer or CLL. That rule meant that I got to hang out in bookstores, at libraries, and on my computer, exploring and learning everything I could about Hilda. My intention was to empower myself enough to take her to task, release her into the wild, and to let go of any ownership or companionship of a permanent nature. (She wasn't family.) I read to learn and then put all the books, the rules, the lessons back on the shelves because we didn't "have" Hilda; nor did she "have" us. She was she, and I was I. We were just together for this day at least, and I would take this step by step, one day at a time.

I was a good girl. (Carol Margaret was raised that way.) Good girls listened to the doctors (and their mothers), put on happy faces, and poured themselves into serving others with graceful self-deprecation in a keeping busy lifestyle with no elephant. Hilda may have moved in, but she didn't define who I was, and I would not allow her to crimp, cramp, or crush my style. I continued with my volunteer activities, organizing my family's activities, tennis, entertaining, and pretending I was superwoman. No ability to fly (darn it!), but if I'd had wings, I'd have been tempted to fly away—except good girls didn't behave with such irresponsibility and abandon. Always I confronted exceptions, and too many competing intentions fostered headaches and heartaches. Why had this complication cluttered and contaminated everything?

Literally and figuratively, the initial doctoring daze led to tremendous gratitude for the power of my imagination. Good ol' Maggie reminded me that imagination can be a great source for spiritual guidance, comfort, and coping. She suggested we pretend that everything was well, that all was perfect, and we were blessed. We started imagining those ideas, and like magic, everything changed into blessing and possibility … except, when it didn't.

One time when this miraculous process didn't work was after a week of chemotherapy. Hilda and I both felt druggy, puffy, bloated, full of steroids and our chemical cocktails, metal mouth, nausea, and all sorts of unsavory sensations. We didn't enjoy eating, we couldn't sleep, and we both felt like climbing the wall in the grossness of being emotionally, physically, and mentally strung out on a precarious limb of yuckiness. I crawled into bed for the weekend after each week's chemo treatment and left Hilda to her own devices until Monday morning and the back to work, back to school, "be happy" mode of operating. We felt so grateful when several weeks later, just before our next week of chemo, we started to feel better. We began to embrace the concept that "it always gets better" with new appreciation.

I pretended the "be happy" part on purpose because, as Maggie said, my most important choice was my attitude. Perhaps I was self-deluded, but I liked to think my family and friends benefitted from my refusal to allow Hilda to conduct or orchestrate my life's music. My ability to be happy and loving was mine. Hilda couldn't steal my choice to be whatever I chose to be. Maggie reminded me that although my chosen behavior was a bit Pollyanna-like, it was a question of what worked at the time, with doctors, friends, family, and ultimately me. The more I tried on an amazing attitude, the less oppressive Hilda seemed, and the closer I grew in my self-acceptance of each living situation I experienced. And eventually, nothing was pretended. I really believed myself, and my survival practices allowed me to thrive—when they worked.

Yet eventually I received the repercussions of my choice when I observed myself drowning in apologies and overly responsible conversations with family, friends, and even Hilda. At least I hope I said "I love you" more than "I'm sorry." It was a close competition for the most-often-repeated phrase. In my ramblings, Hilda compromised my selfhood. I was no longer the captain of the ship, author of the book, keeper of the family … I felt that Hilda was my fault and that because she was with us, I had let down all my relationships. My pleaser nerd took front and center. I felt that if I could make everybody happy, I could be forgiven for having seduced this elephant into hanging out with us. I grew to realize that this attitude was not a happy, efficient, or realistic mode of operating. My smile hid the sadness, disappointment, and horror I felt in my bringing this animal into our home and our family. Not only did I mess up by inviting this elephant into my life, I couldn't seem to get rid of her fast enough. So … I just accelerated the pace, reiterated the apologies and the "I love yous," and did my best to carry on. Maggie gave me a wink and suggested I channel Scarlet O'Hara. "Think about it tomorrow …" And so I did.

Reflections on Doctoring Daze

What I learned in beginning our adventures in treatment was huge for me: I learned that to receive what I choose to experience, I oftentimes get to learn what I don't want, for several reasons. First, when I don't know what I don't know, I get to discover opportunities to educate myself, to observe each situation and from those opportunities, I am open to receive my chosen experience. When I first started learning about doctors, nurses, chemotherapy, and all the festive accoutrements that accompany life with Hilda, I chose to respond from the outside to the inside. What an expert told me, what others said, and how others responded to me guided how I decided to behave and what way of being would support my desired response.

As my experience with trainers and their assistants grew with time and over the years, I learned to trust myself first, by which I mean living from the inside to the outside with my decision- making about treatment and living choices (a.k.a., how to survive and thrive with an elephant in my life). I learned to trust myself by questioning what I experienced. I learned to trust myself because, as Maggie encouraged me, trusting me was like trusting God. I couldn't do one without the other, and both require prayer, she said. So, I practiced trusting myself until it fit like a glove, and I alone decided to whom I proffered that gloved hand in accordance.

I learned to pray all day in every way, and I learned to move past the fear of bad and wrong to good and God, in all times, places, and situations. I got to embrace the idea that while there were many thoughts, ideas, habits, and messages I could clean up, let go, create, and sustain to aid the healing process, many avenues and modalities to explore with treatment, I couldn't really fail. There was only possibility (a.k.a., God), and a mistake was only an opportunity for the grace of learning. And even specialists may not fully appreciate Hilda or understand her or me the way that I could. So, perhaps, I could look at Hilda as a gift? Perhaps she was a present moment package, especially for me, to learn to trust and to connect to what is possible and maybe even wonder-full.

In those early "daze," I deified my oncologist. Newly diagnosed patients often react to their doctor that way, making the doctor the hero of their story. When that reverence, a degree of outside to inside relationship, continues as their partnership grows, I experience that attitude as irresponsible for both parties. Patient-doctor partnership, with patient as "in charge" as much as doctor, is the only one that truly works as far as I can tell. We get to respect and appreciate what each partner brings to the healing process. Any doctor who puts ego and knowledge before honoring relationship with the patient is not operating for the highest good. Good doctoring is more than being right, in control, in charge, the boss. Any doctor who puts his or her reputation and need to be boss before the doctor-patient relationship is a doctor to be avoided. The more I learned, the less my doctor knew, and at one point of the game, I knew more about Hilda than my oncologist did. At that point, it was time for a change.

The same is true with chemo corrals. If nurses and staff look haggard, overworked, and focused on getting through their day so they can get home to other problems, the corral has become like a puppy mill, abusive for all concerned. When nurses are not receiving from their employer and colleagues what they need to thrive, no one benefits. Some physician groups are motivated by higher values than the almighty dollar, and others aren't. When I had friends from my chemo corral die, no one from my trainer's office sent a card, called my friends' families, or showed up at their memorial services.

I asked about that "no show," and I was told by the office manager that they were a for-profit business and couldn't tell their docs or employees how to care for patients and their families. When I offered to set up a care card service (I offered to enroll volunteers to purchase cards, get staff to sign them, and then mail the encouragement or sympathy cards to patients and their families), she showed no interest because my doctor's group was for profit. That saddened me in an unforgettable way.

So too did the overworked staff. They were running intervention for my trainer in a way I couldn't fathom. I would hear him complaining about patients in the back hallway. His voice carried through the entire barn. His staff followed suit. Everyone had their complaints and demons, and that negativity filtered through the chemo corral. When my trainer and his staff moved to another office location, I felt truly hopeful about the change. My father's memorial was etched on the pergola outside the facility, and the offices contained lots of windows and garden views. I had a very dear friend who corralled in a trainer's office in this building, and he said it was grand. My doctor's facility was smaller than the previous one, and the windows were only seen by any staff behind a large, fill-the-room desk. Waiting times were longer, and the staff became harried. My trainer knew and cared less about me and Hilda than he had in the previous decade we'd been together. I wondered how I'd survive the lack of human compassion this place created ... and then Maggie reminded me that we're all on the same boat, and this wasn't Noah's ark. Patients and their animals brought love, opportunities to care, and such compassion to the trainer's staff. And because that staff cared—although they were overworked, burnt out, and underpaid—miracles happened in that short-staffed, crowded, less-than-patient-centered environment, and I could choose to feel grateful and blessed. And so, I did—most of the time. I wanted the environment to be different, the attention to be more individually focused, but this particular trainer's program was a numbers game. Easy to understand why, but not very promising for what I wanted to experience for my healing.

Part of learning about Hilda was also learning about what I, as a patient employing a doctor for my partner, wanted for our healing journey. In future chapters I will discuss some of my healing explorations. There are many, many ways for healing to happen. As my favorite transplant doctors used to say, "Healing is an art, not a science." Although they were talking about stem cell transplants, I would extend the same observation to all forms of healing—physical, mental, emotional, and spiritual. We all get to be artists with our lives. What do I want to paint? What will I write? What song shall I sing? What sculpture do I create with my hands, my heart, and my voice? So much to embrace, to celebrate, to create—why waste time living someone else's story or plan for my life?

CHAPTER 3

Damage Control with Hilda Daze

It's amazing to me how people I knew responded to Hilda's arrival. From shock, grief, and outrage to an overwhelming, overflowing outpouring of love; care and support whooshed in, and I learned the first gift of Hilda: receiving and accepting acts of love that flooded my being like grace. Maggie reminded me to soak it up like a sponge so I could squeeze out the goodness when I dried out and soak up the remnants to share when I was nourished again. Although I rolled my eyes at her corny analogy, it certainly beat stare downs with Hilda.

Family was probably the toughest faction for me to deal with. In my birth family, my only mother began conversation with the repetitive missive, "Oh woe is me! Why does God do this to my children? Why does God do this to me?" My earthly father started toting a flask to Younger Son's little league games, and my younger but taller brother decided to talk to me after a year of silence caused by my expressed concern regarding his alcohol consumption. My Super Sister, bless her heart, had experienced cancer (and our family) the previous year, and she became my number-one go-to support person.

Our home family at that time included my husband, a teenaged son, a preteen son, and a nine-year-old Labrador retriever. Each of their reactions and responses to Hilda were different—ranging from freak out to avoidance to acting out and looking at me as a limited being, soon to be a memory. Not only were all of their responses, feelings, and ways of being different, they kept constantly changing (with the exception of the dog, which remained steadfast and neutral). In witnessing my family's behavior with Hilda, I experienced more angst than I could possibly have imagined. If I were living alone with Hilda, I'd probably have invited her to share a meal together so we could have become friends, or I might have tricked her into leaving me and then rushed to lock every door and window behind her exit.

However, I wasn't alone, and I couldn't run away from Hilda or my guys and the dog. The people closest to me had stopped seeing me as Carol Margaret, Carol, Maggie, or Mom—it was more like poor sick girl/woman … "What can I do for you and Hilda? And," "What's going to happen to me?" Everybody around my home and my family had their own story, and each in some way (except, perhaps, for my sister and the dog) seemed victimized by this Hilda coming to live with me and (by association) them. Maggie tapped me on the shoulder, looked me in the eyes, and said, "You did this. You get to fix it. Get to work."

So … the first thing I learned about the paradox of control was that it is an illusion, a subjective perspective, that it doesn't exist—however tightly I would cling to its illusory power to establish the circumference of my experience. If I did get to be gifted this Health

Imbalance Leukemia Diagnosis Adventure, I would grab it and master it. I would tame it. I would learn everything I could possibly learn about what created my experience, how I could change it, how I could get it to do what I wanted, also known as coexist with me on my terms (peacefully) or send it away forever.

I could search for the strongest parts of me, the corners that could endure anything and survive, the uncaulked crevices of mysterious possibilities I wasn't yet aware of, the walls of shadow and illusion that were only reflections of my own wary projections … I had not yet discovered uncertainty, vulnerability, unknowing, and unfolding as the precious gifts of this adventure, but I was on my way with my intentional plan for my healing. I would face all of these new places within me with courage, compassion, forgiveness, inspiration, and chutzpah because that's what "damage control" with Hilda was all about. It would be quite a ride, but I was going to take this trip one growth in awareness at a time until I could leap forward with the surety that there was no such thing as control.

And so my plan evolved into this something I created. Maggie reminded me of the most important behaviors in mastering Hilda: personal responsibility, prayer, and thanksgiving (not necessarily in that order). With those additions, my personal damage control with Hilda began.

As for damage control with family, what can I say? I'd learned through earlier experiences to meet people where I perceived them to be. With my only mother, I continued to be the good, obedient daughter, rallying like a trooper with a smile, superficial, happy health reports, and what often was inauthentic personal/nonpersonal expression. I ignored my earthly father's new accessory, and I rejoiced that my younger but taller brother was in relationship with me again, careful to do or say nothing to disturb our newfound peace. My Super Sister was supportive in awesome ways, a rock star for me. So was the dog, totally unconditional, and I felt so grateful.

My One Husband had a lot going on for him personally at this time, and that is his story to relate as he chooses. All I can share about his and my sons' responses to Hilda are solely from my own perspective of their experience. That said, my experience of my husband's response to my diagnosis was that he felt afraid, frustrated, impatient, confused, and totally all over the board. I owned a very over-responsible need to "control" all of his/our chaos. My solution was to keep him from going to treatments with Hilda and me. I also thought to distract him by suggesting fun and bonding times he might share with our boys, activities he especially enjoyed, like fishing in Canada and backpacking Appalachian Trail. I kept up my same full schedule and activity level and only rested on weekends after treatment at the corral or when no one (except for the dog) was home with Hilda and me.

Elder Son was a teenager, had a job, was almost driving, played football, and was a tender, caring, and open guy. He came up with creative and loving ideas and gestures of care and service and became discouraged when his dad and brother tagged onto what he'd made as his unique contributions. I saw a spark dim in him as he became part of a trio and could only find his own niche by separating himself from the tribe and keeping his feelings to himself. I felt guilty for Hilda's presence and the disruption she brought to his teenage years, a time that, in my opinion, the majority of kids get to be all about themselves.

Almost twelve-year-old Younger Son was in the throes of his own adolescence at the time and chose to provide support for his father unconditionally—a real gift—and he stayed in his own experience (which was not particularly easy, a.k.a., puberty) at the time. It was such a blessing to me that he continued to be who he was through the ups and downs of Hilda and repercussions in our family.

So with my guys, I got to tiptoe and shape-shift until I didn't or couldn't anymore. The guilt, blame, and responsibility I placed on myself for my judgment on their experiences of Hilda and me were no service to any of them or to me. When I awakened one morning, it was like a cloud lifted, and I saw clearly that my control/judgment/interpretation was all make-believe. "Everything is perfect, all of the time." Maggie chortled.

I began to recognize the differences between being responsible for my experience and being responsible for others' experience. Being responsible for me includes not blaming me or projecting my blame or anger onto others around me. Being responsible for me means recognizing and honoring that others' opinions of me are none of my business, and that how they interpret or respond to me or to Hilda is none of my business as well. And that applies to family as well as everyone else. Very freeing those differences are. Yippee!

Damage control for me includes honoring myself as a work in progress and accepting myself in whatever condition I'm in. Dealing with what is, I pray. I choose a vision for what I dream and hold true, my vision of what I want for my life. Then I get to choose to be whatever feels congruent to my support of that dream. I pray again, and this time I say, "Thank you! My vision already is!" And so it is.

That's pure damage control in a nutshell. "Thank you, God!" Maggie nods with a knowing smile. "And that's the stuff of miracles," I say, giggling gleefully as we do a happy dance with the dog.

CHAPTER 4

A Post-Daze Look at a Pre-Hilda Daze Haze

Once upon a time...

That phrase is a magical start to a great story. As a young woman, I still believed in fairy tales, and in my best and brightest daze, Maggie always reminds me that a vivid imagination shortens a challenging tribulation. There I was in my late twenties, an inspired, joy-filled mother of two sons and wife of One Husband, living my dream and loving my family. A significant chapter in my becoming storyline was the expansion of our family through the procreation and delivery of more incredible children. This desire, this dream, this delightful part of my favorite fairytale wasn't possible because something was wrong with *me*. Figuring out the whys didn't work, and nothing made sense. (Maggie reminds me that a life dream often experiences that conditionality before it resolves or evolves into something else.)

The "good, forever, and irreplaceable doctor" (a.k.a., my OB-GYN) suggested that, perhaps, something more was at work with my body after three failed attempts to grow babies in my womb. In my visits to the good, forever, and irreplaceable doctor, I discovered that my babies' hearts were still, they had died within me without my consent or awareness, and our only option became a delivery from my womb to their tombs. I felt so sad. My good, forever, irreplaceable doctor referred me to the specialists who eliminated many potential diagnoses to finally uncover Hilda, responsible, perhaps, for the heartbreaks I experienced before I even met her.

The autoimmune, strange, and deceptive illnesses I suffered for years before CLL diagnosis brought hospitalizations for fevers and crippling pains. I had treatments for mysterious travails that appeared, asserted themselves, and then snuck away in the dark to gather their cohorts to visit me when I least expected visitors. As these "animals" would come and then go, I would ask myself, "Were they ever really here? Did this truly happen? What was this?" and no one really ever diagnosed or understood my experience conclusively. Maggie suggested we could entertain ourselves like Nancy Drew in *the case of the inside out, upside down, really crazy lady.*

The death of a dream- to grow and nourish more souls in this world- was the most challenging limitation and loss I had faced thus far in my life. From that loss/limitation, I learned to reinvent myself, to create another vision for my life. I realized that not all of life's events were to be grasped or fully understood. I am blessed that I get to witness, embrace, and release one moment into the next. And … a part of me feels lost, fragile, tired, and fiercely determined to bulldoze forward in all outward-focused activities: super-mom, super-wife, super-volunteer … smile on face, hide the vulnerability, mask the pain, and move on.

I didn't know what I didn't know, and at the same time, I knew nothing. Maggie encouraged me to give myself time and to create loving, healing rituals to recover myself in joy. She also encouraged me to broaden my definition of family and what nurturing could look like. Most of all, she taught me how to reframe my thoughts, feelings, and experience into something I could embrace as a gracious creation of possibility. I would not have survived this time of painful growth without Maggie's heart. God bless Maggie!

Post Daze Haze Reflection

Death happens all the time. It hurts because we love or become attached to what dies—an idea, a dream, a fairytale, a person, a pet … Yet because all truth is paradox, we must "die" to be born into what we are called to become.

Out of every loss comes some kind of gift, which we often can only discern with time after any death. Life is birthed from the ashes. ("Like a phoenix," Maggie exclaims.)

Sometimes I wonder about our failure to embrace, to truly grieve and cleanse our hearts of the pain, separation, and longing we feel with a death—our inability to express the subjective hell we create for ourselves when we ignore healing practices. Does not doing the healing work bring greater pain and greater opportunities for the undead yet dying parts of ourselves to drape the windows and lock the doors of our souls? Can the light that releases the separation and the longing be able or allowed to enter?

Once upon a time … is a present moment phrase in every moment. It's the only time there is. Always, a start to a miracle is just around the corner. And sometimes "time" is infinite. Sometimes, it flies. *And* it gets to be included in all of our stories for all time as it represents our relationships to *all* and *everything.*

The Downs

INTRODUCTION

So many of my "once upon a times" boil *down* to a seemingly profound simplicity of a sacred spiritual something, a something I choose to embrace as my truth until I break *down* into another moment that contains a new spiritual nugget for me to embrace as a different truth. Competing, more or less justifiable beliefs, truths, ideas … constantly changing and unfolding into somethings I don't recognize before the moment they appear. Growing my awareness is an up-and-*down* process for me, with lots of highs and lows.

Although control is an illusion, I often get caught up in my desire to get everything *down* and settled so I can create a master plan/composition and get everything right (like an A or in perfect order, measure, time, and tempo). Then something like Hilda comes into my life, and I get knocked *down* from the podium where, with great aplomb, I'm conducting my masterpiece symphony of *Carol Margaret Hohlfelder Roth* (in A major). ("How humbling," Maggie whispers with compassion.)

When I pick myself up and dust myself off ("A saint is just a sinner who falls down and gets up!" Maggie cheers me on when I do the up and *down* thing.), I oftentimes find myself choosing to get *down* to doing my work, settling *down* to allow the time, space, and grace to learn how to create the first *downs* that will advance my saint-want-to-be-self *down* the field in this game we call "life."

When an event like Hilda ("Just use the actual word, Carol," says an eye-rolling Carol Margaret.) ... When something like *cancer* or imbalance of any kind approaches, confronts, invades, infiltrates, castrates, blocks, or tackles anyone I've ever known, heard of, and loved, it brings overwhelmingly numerous moments of *downs*. Attempts to master the beast, rise above circumstance, transcend the pain and the feeling that failure of self-control or ignorance was the source; every progressive growth in awareness, for every healing avenue traveled, there are ups and *downs*. And to become a leader in my life ("Lead people, manage results," Carol Margaret pontificates.), I get to figure out how to create what I want. What I was experiencing with Hilda when she first arrived and I was getting to know her was what I didn't want.

I wanted to wave my magic miracle wand and say, "*Cancer! Be gone!*" ("And so it is!" Maggie clapped.)

It was time to get *down* and into the game ...

CHAPTER 5

Getting Down to Get Down

After the first daze of CLL and what it brought to me and my world, I realized that, when the newness of this Hilda wore off, I would need to get down to the "nitty gritty" of this creature and determine her significance in my life. I could orchestrate a plan, but as I reminded myself, plans have a way of not always working. I found myself conversing with God, via Maggie. She and God suggested I give up the need to be right and in control; my inclination to judge, interpret, and compare; my need to understand; and my impatience with all of it. God also told Maggie to tell me that if I could detach from my experience enough to live in the questions, choose to trust in goodness and miracles as part of a holy life, and learn to embrace gratitude for everything (or at least pretend to be thankful until I became grateful), then my learning, loving, and desired experience could be really gracious, generous, and full of possibility. In other words, my choices, my attitude, my willingness to embrace and accept *cancer* in my life could lift me up from the *downs* and perhaps give me the wings to fly.

So I prayed. I researched information about possible physical, mental, emotional, spiritual, and metaphysical reasons for Hilda's presence in my life. Much of what I learned challenged me at first. As I spent more time growing my awareness about what I could do to speed Hilda's farewell, it actually created in me more questions than answers and stretched me further than I could have imagined. Soon I learned what resonated as true for me and what didn't.

I explored different modalities of healing. I had spent my early years as a traditional Midwest Methodist who trusted Western medicine and all the doctors whose practices served me and my family. One of the gifts of *cancer* was learning about complementary and alternative healing therapies, metaphysics, diet, Eastern medicine, acupuncture, herbal supplements, yoga, tai chi, and so forth. From May of 1998 until March of 2012, I garnered a leukemia diagnosis a long time to live with an elephant! During those almost fourteen years, I may have explored every healing technique, art, or potential cure for CLL, and I learned so much about me, Hilda, and all of creation around me. When I really got *down* to *it*, "*it*" was all connected. I learned to trust myself first and I trusted myself to discern whom or what to trust. Choosing to trust myself was the first hallmark of my healing journey. Unless I learned to trust myself, I would never be able to embrace trusting the possibilities, the miracles of God, and a life of alchemy.

I experimented with many modalities of healing. Faith healers, certain diets, cleanses, intuitive classes, reiki, hands-on prayer, healing touch, akashic records, acupuncture, Chinese medicine, herbal supplements, yoga … those were only a few. Some I loved—I became a reiki master and a healer for others. I took intuitive classes and learned to channel for guidance and spiritual direction. I learned what foods inspired my healing and which didn't. I learned that healing is not an "either/or" -not Eastern, Western medicine *or* Native American-, but an "*and*," and that my life gets to be inclusive of all that serves wholeness, wellness, restoration, balance, and goodness. This process of living the questions for optimal healing can be quite fun, sometimes tough, maybe uncomfortable, always open to change, embracing or discarding what works or doesn't. I think now about how ridiculous some of my experiments were and how life-affirming others were. Some choices put me in precarious situations health wise, but I've survived to tell the story, and it was all part of my healing/learning/loving. I feel very grateful. Maggie nods with appreciation, and we give each other a big hug.

Reflections on Getting Down to Get Down

New stuff isn't always easy with a large and uncomfortable animal like Hilda in residence. To make necessary changes, accommodating her condition and presence in my life when everything in my world had shifted, felt overwhelming. While I chose to treat *cancer* as an adventure most of the time, there were also times I wanted to pull the covers over my head, close my eyes, and pretend this whole experience was merely a nightmare.

In a way, it was. My mantra, from my Hilda experience and every other experience so far, is that *no matter what—it always gets better!*

So a bad day is simply a bad day. With patience, and when I remember, reviewing all those things God via Maggie told me (on a bad day, I am not always intentionally mindful with my retention skills)—things to give up—like judgment, comparison, interpretation, attachment, the assumptions that I'm right or in control (and so on …) a bad day can disappear into a miracle. As I saturate my being, fully wallowing into a bad day, I can know deep *down*, it will be better sometime. I will get through whatever I'm going through. I get to trust myself that I can lead myself out of whatever situation I'm in, and if I need help, there's always God, Maggie, and even Jesus, Ganesh (Hilda likes that one!), Buddha, or my pastor, Carolyn. I can be grateful after the nightmare that it's over. Or I can wonder, as I often did, "Was it ever real or did it happen?" "I love to wonder, don't you?" Maggie gazes into the sky as she points to a cloud that is perfectly shaped like an elephant.

CHAPTER 6

Settling Down

Once upon a time stories often include a part, ideally at the end of a tale, but sometimes found scattered throughout the adventure, some resolution period, a time of settling down and making peace, reconciled harmony and a semblance of routine. Although my particularly settled moments were intermittent, due to a plethora of chaotic elements and bizarre creatures presenting themselves arbitrarily during Hilda's residence, it did contain holy moments of absolute grace. For those moments I grew especially grateful. Knowing that these magical moments could surprise me and be prevalent in my storyline at one time or another brought me confidence through hope.

By "hope" I don't mean a "maybe kind of wistful wish." Hope, to me, is a conscious choice to connect to possibility ("To God!" Maggie gently corrects me). Hope is prayer. Hope is vision. Hope is the miracle wand of accepted grace. Hope is choosing to create a mantra of healing. Hope is choosing to believe that *everything* gets better no matter what, that what will be already is somehow, and I get to be thankful.

Carol Margaret suggested I could be confusing aspects of hope with faith. When we got Maggie involved, we mutually concluded that the present moment power of possibility includes trust, love, and hope/connection. So when I settle down, I trust myself and God, I love myself and God, and I connect to myself and God. Maggie reminds me that I am one with all creation, which means trusting, loving, and connecting to me is doing the same with every other living thing and bringing all I am to my every experience.

When initial chemotherapy treatment began, it was new and confusing. A couple of years into the process, I knew what to expect, for the most part, and grew used to the routine I experienced with doctors' offices and the chemo corral. I knew what my symptoms would be when I needed treatment because Hilda would always bellow and blow when it was time to subdue her. I was old hat at the corral, and nothing seemed to daunt me. I knew the players, the game, and the program—until I didn't—but when it was easy, it was easy. When it wasn't easy, I got to reboot via my learning curve. Change was an absolute constant in every single experience. I began to discern that perhaps adapting and flowing with the change was an opportunity for learning and healing, and that my feeling secure and comfortable with my routine was simply another illusion of control with a safety net. Very thankful I was that I always could choose to hope, to know beyond a doubt that no matter what, we would get through anything, like plugging a cord into a power source. Thank you, God! And thank you, Wayne Dyer, for suggesting that visual spiritual solution!

At the same time that I was learning the ropes of living with a chronic creature, the rest of my life was providing more opportunities for hope. Marital problems, parenting and relationship issues in regard to teenager challenges, family illnesses, changes in residence, financial flux, and deaths of dearly loved ones ... seemingly unending amounts of havoc, change, and opportunities to choose hope.

An opportunity to choose hope doesn't mean I actually plugged in the cord—it merely means it was available for my use. I learned that suffering is a choice sometimes because hope is always available. Key is the "just do it" thing. Maggie said that perhaps all of my immersion in the painful suffering and drama of my primary relationships was perhaps a gift empowering me to relegate Hilda to the bedroom closet for a much-needed time out. To this day, I'm not 100 percent positive every tumultuous experience during the Hilda years was a desired gift, but I know that when I made choices to actively vision, love, pray, let go, and trust ... everything always got better. And Hilda didn't seem as important. She was part of my experience, but when these other hurdles blocked my bridges, she was only another obstacle to clear, and I knew it all would settle down eventually.

Settling down might be like going to the mat in yoga. My practice of yoga has been up and down over the years. When I go to my mat, yoga is the all and only in that moment. No matter what goes on around me, I can choose to flow. I can choose to be present. I can honor what my body, mind, and spirit need. I can choose congruence. I can align my chosen way of being with what possibility/God is for me. My response does not need to be reaction based. Rather, it is my gift to my present experience. "How hopeful!" Maggie encourages me with a slight smile as we meet together in downward dog.

Reflections on Settling Down

To truly "settle" down without any cursory illusion resolution requires being so present in the moment that I detach from my experience and live my vision and prayer as a calm oasis of the healer I am. Practically and realistically, it requires concerted discipline, consistent practice, and the exercise of balance, and flexibility.

Before Hilda, I practiced yoga, and my body could move in ways that Hilda's advancement hindered. I loved balance and flexibility poses. When I returned to yoga after my stem cell transplant, it was not the same body that returned to my mat—I wobbled and wondered where my old body had gone. I began to begin again—to let go of my expectations for myself, to die/end comparisons with what was, to rebirth into the newness of my new body, my open mind, my precious yoga in each present moment. I'm learning to accept what is and choose joy in my practice, with my subtle improvements and with my painful struggles. I'm learning to settle down into my practice with immense gratitude that I'm here, now, and … "Namaste," Maggie interrupts me as she grabs my soapbox, mat in hand, and we scurry off to class. I've learned that settling down is temporary and merely a pause in the action. Thank you, Life.

CHAPTER 7

Down And Out

So as the years went by, Hilda and I developed a method of maneuvering with each other that seemed to work for us—we graced each other with enough space to artfully coexist as we grazed and gazed together in a state of mutual tolerance and a grudgingly respectful disdain for our cohabitation.

As I watched Hilda and grew to know her over the years, it dawned on me that, perhaps, it could be within my power to banish her from the sovereign kingdom of Carol Margaret Hohlfelder Roth. All the experimenting I'd done in regard to healing ideologies, theologies, and modalities, I brought to the purveyance table as I prepared to escort Hilda to a new destination far from me. I would no longer coddle her or allow her the freedom and space I'd bestowed to keep the peace. It was time to be a bit feisty, so I put Carol Margaret in charge.

And (I'm still not sure how she really did it.), Carol Margaret utilized every part of her tool kit and spirited Hilda to the great abyss. To this day, Maggie and I don't know where that place was. Perhaps we didn't care. Maggie said my desire to know and understand the "hows" after the fact was irrelevant. We celebrated because Hilda was free, and so were we! For four years, we felt on top of the world in regard to our emancipation from Hilda's presence. We proclaimed to the world that Hilda had departed; Carol Margaret Hohlfelder Roth was cured, healed, and reborn! Praise the Lord! We danced around the kitchen, took on new adventures with joy and determination, and rallied around all the vibrantly clean, green pastures of our stomping grounds minus an elephant! No more visits to doctors! No more sympathy and encouragement cards or meals brought in by thoughtful, well-meaning friends that I could never pay back during chemo weeks. My friends no longer brought pity, plastic smiles, or the need to notice or comment on my appearance, fragility, or attitude. My two sons got to be teenagers again. My One Husband seemed happy. Our animals (we now had two young Labrador retrievers and two inherited cats) danced with us through every room in the house. No more paying the doctor for what I already knew! No more chemotherapy! We were giddy with joy! "Yippee" was our "cowabunga" creed, and blessing and happiness were ours to seize and celebrate because Hilda had disappeared. It wasn't just "for now"; it was "forever." Carol Margaret convinced us.

To get to this place, I focused extensively on what thoughts would inspire healing. I learned that inspiration fueled the love I am and allowed me to be joyful. I learned to seek inspiration in every moment—except when I didn't. When I did follow the direction of my dreams for my life and dreamed big dreams, I became expansive, courageous, and transcendent of my experience. I found so much joy in even thinking about all the possibilities that I decided to choose to live in that ever-present gracious space where all things are possible.

To experience appreciation and thanksgiving for the gift of amazing connection to spirit and possibility, I also got to learn its antithesis. It's very easy not to choose to be inspired and joyful when I feel miserable physically. It's also challenging when I'm confronting things I don't embrace in my life, "the victim/victimizing conversations/experiences," Carol Margaret calls them. Sometimes I got to "practice" to remember my power of choice in my every experience.

But in the moment, that entire four-year moment, I celebrated, my soul sang, and I lived a life as large as I knew how to muster!

During that period, which occurred after more than several dearly loved ones (my porch-swinging grandmother, my earthly father, my younger but taller brother, some tried and true friends, and the original Roth Labrador retriever) died, I took risks and tried new experiences to learn, grow, and have fun, in spite of whatever fear or pain knocked on my door. None of them were medically related to me personally, which was an enormous boon to my spirit. So much of my life after diagnosis and before this disease-free period was spent with aspects of sadness and suffering lurking around every corner. It took every fiber of strength and faith I could extract just to keep my equilibrium, and often I fell down and painstakingly picked myself up. ("Like a saint!" insists Maggie, who always looks for the possibilities in everyone, including me.)

Part of my soul song during this period was accelerated caregiving for family, friends, causes, and crusades I passionately loved. I had this dis-ease free body, and I had so much to do!

No doctor had diagnosed this healthy state of my body, mind, and spirit. It was a state of being I intuitively knew as true for me. My singing joyfully soul created workshops, classes, community groups, sacred, holy, and family/friend gatherings. My soul song wrote, prayed, sang, spoke, listened, and created what I felt called to manifest. Spirit was guide, director, and creator, and I was humbled, awed, and thankful for the direction, grace, and purpose I was following and accepting as who and what I chose to be. Thank, you God!

My moment was a four-year moment, and then I woke up one day with a high fever, total hearing loss, and a wretched sinus infection. An attempt to restore my hearing by putting tubes in my ears couldn't be done because my hemoglobin was dangerously low. That failed attempt happened on my birthday that year and put me back in the hospital. My irritated oncologist told me this health failure was my fault, insisting that with regular visits, I wouldn't be in such an imbalanced place. My good, forever, irreplaceable doctor referred me to an ear, nose, and throat doctor after scolding me for having gone to a med check instead of finding a primary care physician. Everyone seemed to find me disappointing, appointing me as the misaligned source of this manifested turbulence. My two sons and One Husband were unhappy, even forlorn. My only mother was upset that I couldn't hear her voice on the phone telling me "happy birthday," and my sole reassurance was the appearance of my ultimate infectious disease doc, whose very presence always made everything better.

One of the biggest pieces I had yet to grasp, one of my more challenging ideas to embrace with this debacle, would soon arrive. Ending up in this hospital bed was one thing. What entered the room with the doctors and nurses was the familiar nagging recognition of something else … With grand aplomb, Hilda cavorted into the room, waving her trunk as if to say, "You couldn't lose me if you tried! I'm back!" Carol Margaret grimaced and stared her down. When that didn't work, she put her hands over her face and sobbingly admitted, "We did something wrong. She found us again. This is our fault. She's back, and I don't think she's ever going away. What will become of us?" Maggie was already on her knees praying as I pulled the hospital blanket over my head, willing myself to think happy thoughts beyond the horrific drama I witnessed in this new moment. "*Happy birthday*" to me! And so, our reunion began in earnest …

We thought we'd "gotten down" to a life without a Hilda. Maggie kept repeatedly humming "Bridge over Troubled Water" (a favorite of hers), and the lyrics that kept coming to my mind repeatedly were "When you're down and out …" I was down with Hilda again, out of my comfort zone, and this time she had grown larger, older, less competent, kind of odiferous, and a bit senile.

Taking care of her would be a different ball game this time around, and I'd need to be at the top of my game to take her to the goal line. I felt devastatingly low, at the bottom of the barrel. Talk about failed endeavors, fallacious expectations, imaginative delusions … I felt bad, wrong, stupid, and utterly defeated.

More prayer, more study, more courage … This time around Hilda had brought other needy animal buddies with her, lots of nagging and annoying irritations, seasoned with arduously complex complications. The ultimate infectious disease doc would get to be our hero over and over and over again.

TGIF (today gratitude is first) became Maggie's suggestion for combatting the down and outs. "When we go in and up, everything gets better," she expressed with conviction. We started every day praying thank you for everything, claiming and naming our blessings. When the discipline of gratitude became daunting, Carol Margaret took control. "Practice!" she ordered sternly. Because I was deaf for a period of time, I could be still and know the silence of my soul song. When I couldn't hear, I didn't talk as much, which I am certain my One Husband appreciated. When my hearing returned, I could be especially grateful because I'd had this wonderful opportunity to rest in the silence, and my One Husband could be happy to, once again, not listen to me. "Practice listening!" Carol Margaret lectures him as he leaves the room.

Healing and treatment that year were continuous. IV antibiotics, pic lines, bone marrow biopsies, chemotherapy, transfusions, infusions, treatment for unrelenting complications, imbalance in everything. Weekly chemo from February through September, immunoglobulin therapy … All of this sandwiched between my One Husband's father's death and my only mother's death. All I seemed to have time and opportunity for that year were treatment, response to treatment, prayer, caregiving, and damage control. Steroids helped with the prayer part. Prayer became my favorite conscious activity when I couldn't sleep, which was almost all of the time, and the gift of this experience was that I could pray without ceasing. ("Another thing to be grateful for!" Maggie says, winking.)

Little did I suspect that year what an enormous and permanently attached fixture Hilda had stubbornly decided to be. I couldn't leave the room without her bellowing and braying. When she got angry with me, she blocked my passage to anywhere other than where she wanted me to stay. This was so different from the early years when we gave each other sporadic breathing room, if not in every single moment, at least occasionally. The activities I had relished, like sharing stories, adventures, and memories with my recently deceased younger but taller brother's son, were abandoned because Hilda's demands left me no time for my elder nephew. Fewer trips to make memories with my dying only mother and more cries for attention to be heard and addressed in my everyday family life. Less energy for the exercise and social activities with friends I loved. Life became surviving the down and outs by going in and up, staying with what was in front of me in each moment of the every day. One day at a time (again), and just enough light for the step I'm on. Breathe. Breathe. Breathe.

"When pain is all around, like a bridge over troubled water, I will lay me down ..." Maggie sings soulfully. "Thank you, Maggie." I wipe at my watery eyes. "No. Thank you, Jesus!" Maggie closes her eyes, swept away in the music.

CHAPTER 8

Down and Up

As one year led to another, the nagging, annoying irritations and arduously complex complications trailing Hilda competed with my ability to function in my preferred mode of operating like my heroines from childhood: Pollyanna, Elsie Dinsmore, and Julie Andrews. Hilda was incorrigible, and accompanying her this time came insect-like creatures and slimy characters like warts, rashes, infections, hemolytic anemia, ITP, neutropenia, arthritis, and fatigue; opportunities for an abundance of time spent in my ever-constant love/hate relationship with prednisone, transfusions, drugs, allergic reactions, hospitalizations, infusions, and the always prevalent personal relationship challenges Hilda seemed to draw out of the woodwork, fabrics, walls, windows, and floors of my life. Everything seemed more overwhelming this time around, and I often forgot to hope. Sometimes I didn't even smile. Why had CLL returned to me? "Don't even start about the no answer to why questions!" I chastised Maggie when she started to open her mouth.

What I experienced was what I thought I had earlier overcome and mastered, and as I was forced to embrace my lessons, I knew that every time I think I have arrived, there's another track to travel to get to discover more—an even greater awareness—of the same lessons. Once again, beginner's mind, and I don't know what I don't know. To reframe that awareness for this next chapter of my adventure … a beginner's heart and I know that I don't know. I get to peel away the drapes, unlock the doors, maybe open the windows and let the light, the breeze, and the discovery inside of me. "And be grateful!" Maggie preaches. This time I nod my head in agreement, and I forgive myself for all of my judgment, doubt, dismay, and despair. It is time for beginning again.

First on my docket was dealing with all the relationship stuff that came up for healing … My One Husband had bought a big business in a small town almost three hours away and put money, time, and energy into it and other real estate ventures. Elder Son was now a graduated, successfully employed adult and living far away from us. Younger Son was a now a twenty-something independently excelling at life in college. Super Sister, the only living member of my birth family, and I were dealing with our now-dead only mother's estate issues, and life included more travel, increased change, and erratic flux on a personal level for me. And as Carol Margaret reminds me, I cannot ever forget our two eccentrically demanding inherited cats and two creatively charming, large, and adorable adolescent Labrador retrievers, always lovingly requiring attention that must be paid. "Rather zoo—eee …" Maggie has that glint in her eye again as I roll my eyes at her attempt to be humorous.

We bought a lake cottage on a lake close to the business One Husband had purchased in his home town two and a half hours away. We traveled to Europe for an awesome vacation. We hosted a wonderful family reunion for our remaining family. We went on fun trips to closer destinations. So many really amazing dreams were realized in spite of my experiencing less than optimal physical health. Infinite blessings for which we celebrated thanksgiving were such a gift! I felt really happy—except when I didn't.

Finances changed in the Roth household. To maintain our real estate holdings and to avert bankruptcy, we used the entire significant amount we'd inherited from my dead only mother. We realized that to keep the business in One Husband's home town solvent, we needed to move up there to run it. We put our family home on the market and moved into a rental house in One Husband's hometown (the lake house was too tiny for all our "stuff"). We stored or gave away the furniture, assorted and random things that didn't fit in our space or for this chapter in our lives, and moved north with resolve to meet this financial challenge head on.

One Husband was totally immersed in our financial survival. In the meantime, I used my life's events as an excuse to avoid responsibility for my health. The change and drama around me drew all of my attention and involvement. I created a lot of worry for myself—would I find friends, create community, find doctors, and discover my life in this little town of my One Husband's? In the meantime, the economy continued to flail, and our home wasn't selling. We ended up renting it to what seemed like a nice family who said they wanted to buy it. They agreed to care for it as if it were their own, until they could buy it. Our rental house up north was great, except it had bats, mice, squirrels, raccoons, and rabbits and we had two inherited cats and two adolescent Labrador retrievers who had no idea what to do with any of these exciting creatures, inside and outside our rental home. It was entertaining and full of havoc. And the biggest thing was … my health wasn't getting better. I could ignore it. I could pretend I was happy, well-adjusted, and feeling terrific, but I wasn't. I felt crummy. I missed my friends, my kids, my dead only mother … and I needed to find a new approach to health care because my docs were all far away. Time to buckle down and create an attitude that would lift me up out of the gloom to the place, space, and grace where healing happens. I had to get down to the business of cheering up, looking up, and being aligned with possibility again. "We better pray and listen," Maggie ardently proposed as we held hands and got down on our knees.

One Husband and I had explored all kinds of alternative and complementary health care options for wellness. The little town where we lived had a center that offered acupuncture and Chinese medicine. I figured it could be worth a try, and for a while I found it helpful with my new stressors and with augmenting my physical wellbeing. I also did research and received a referral to an integrative cancer center in a large city less than two hours away from the little town in which we lived. This center was holistic, offered yoga classes, diet guidance, physical therapy, massage, cutting edge medicine; and the founders had written books about integrative cancer treatments. I became enthused about them, and when I couldn't put off dealing with Hilda any longer -she smelled so bad and brayed with such volume, I couldn't even hide her in the garage-, I scheduled an appointment to drive the almost two hours to see their team of doctors.

These new doctors could not believe Hilda's condition and chastised me (and my previous trainer) for being remiss in my treatment of her. They recommended new drugs, new therapy, and another new way to eat, move, and breathe during treatment. The treatment rooms were private, with windows and photographs of birch and fir trees on the walls. Cooking classes would occur during chemo. I was invited to attend, and if I didn't, they came by my room and offered samples. One Husband enjoyed that part of our time there. I was invited to yoga class or perhaps a massage during chemotherapy—very different than what I'd experienced with my previous oncologist.

The only thing I can say about chemotherapy is this: chemo is chemo, no matter what! Drugs, drugs, drugs flooding my system—hopefully for the highest good and the removal of elephantitis from my physical person—but chemotherapy is the induction of foreign chemicals into my imbalanced body to break the cancer down so that my body can rebalance in a new way. The process is somewhat violent, necessary at this point in my healing adventure, and a process that kills before it births. To follow a protocol like this integrative center wanted and eat the prescribed foods when I had nausea, metal mouth, constipation, and insomnia wasn't what I wanted to do. For years before, I had been grateful to eat anything that tasted good or I could keep down. These people wanted me to avoid my comfort foods, to attend classes and support groups during treatment times—new concepts for me. The things I relished about chemotherapy sessions were my music, One Husband, a good book, my journal, and a nap. This new center wanted to tweak a methodology that had worked for me for a long time. I considered what I wanted and what would bring the highest level of healing for me.

My personal goal during treatment was to get through it, whatever it took. When treatment was behind me was when I would cleanse and choose a macrobiotic or vegetarian diet for a period of time. I chose what was for my highest good based on my learning and experience, and I trusted myself. One of the founders of this treatment center came in my room for one of my treatments and pleaded with me to follow all of their protocol. I graciously declined and felt congruent with my choice. I duly considered what she said and believed. Would I have chosen my own direction over an "authority's" opinions earlier in my Hilda years? Doubtful at best ... At this point I became responsible for what I chose with my health care, right, wrong, good, or bad. "There's no right, wrong, or bad, Carol," Maggie shares with me. "You're so good, Maggie." What else could I say and be right?

So the further we travailed with Hilda, the more familiar, authentic, eccentric, and aware I became. I knew what I thought I knew. I trusted my intuition, imagination, and possibility. I knew I didn't know it all or even a little piece of the puzzle. I trusted that my vision of healing was real and true and that whatever I experienced in any given moment was sourced from a place of future transformation. No matter what, when everything seemed bad, it would get better. When I soared on top of the world, I would need to land for a bathroom break. The highs and lows, the peaks and valleys were adventures to be chosen, embraced, and transformed into the dream I desired for my life. "Response-ability," Carol Margaret emoted. It brought another level of gamesmanship to this Hilda thing, and I felt up for the challenge—except when I didn't.

The long trips to the integrative cancer center in the large town necessitated overnight stays for two consecutive days of chemotherapy each month. Each month I received at least two, usually more, units of blood transfused at the local hospital in our little town. My blood type was O negative, the universal donor. I often thought, as I received the blessing of donated blood, about how much I wished

I could donate blood to others and felt sad I'd never receive the gift of that blessing. Maggie reminded me to be grateful for the huge blessing I received by the donation of others' blood to me. I paused in the immense grace and gratitude of the realization that life is lived in what is, can, and will be: the "I *ams*," as Maggie calls them. "Don't get caught in the what isn't, can't, and won't be. The 'I am *nots*' tie you up in knots!" Maggie passionately remarks. I am blessed, no matter what! One Husband likes to talk about sponsoring thoughts as intentions for vision. "A re-sponsored thought!" I clap my hands in delight at his inspiration for possibility-sponsored intentions to rearrange my mind's knots into the gracious untangling of grateful "I *ams*."

CHAPTER 9

Giving Up to Get Down:

One Husband and I, our two adolescent Labrador retrievers, and our one of two inherited cats -Younger Son having adopted the elder cat.-decided to store or give away the rest of our furniture and simplify our living and finances by relocating to our tiny 480-square-foot cottage on the lake. We knew it would be crowded, tight quarters for all of us, but it seemed the only way we could focus on our physical, emotional, and financial healing. All six of us, including Hilda, could share meditation time every morning and evening with extraordinary lake views, and for this beauty, we were truly grateful. The dogs loved swimming in the lake, barking at the neighbors, and attempting to eat the cat food and kitty litter. The cat creatively practiced all of the many ways she could taunt the dogs into misbehavior mode. Our home was closer to One Husband's business, so he could take his workaholic tendencies to a new extreme, justifying longer work days as a response to the chaotic activities of our tiny cottage's menagerie. I did the best I could with the chaos. Maggie reminded me to be still, breathe, be grateful, and

CAROL M. H. ROTH

pray. The cottage seemed an easier place for me to maintain some semblance of order, as I grew weaker and developed complications and infections from treatment, in spite of treatment, and even from lack of treatment. I was going nowhere quickly, and I couldn't figure out how to stop the downward spiral.

My current trainers in the large city two hours from our small town had just published a book and were asking patients to refrain from calling their answered phone line because they were so popular with the public and press. Instead patients were encouraged to leave a message on a recorded line, where messages would be returned in twenty-four hours. If it were an emergency, patients could call the answered line, but were told to expect long wait times due to high call volume. The only option for emergency calls was to go to the hospital in our small town and hope that our local doctors could connect with the trainers in the large city two hours away from the hospital in our small town. All my many and constant blood transfusions were in this hospital in our small town, and although the transfusions seemed to go well, the small town's hospital did not inspire the confidence I experienced with those treatment centers to which I was accustomed. It was time, once again, to change things up.

However, at this point in my Hilda adventure, I was not seeing possibility in any Western, Eastern, or complementary medicine methodology or techniques. I kept up treatments with traditional Chinese medicine and would check in with the trainers in the large town two hours away from our small town, but it was rather discouraging at best. The Chinese medicine provider thought I was improving. The nutritionist thought the cleanses she recommended were helpful, even though I became very thin and felt very sick.

The acupuncturist suggested I practice patience and mastery of my health through his preferred practices. When my hemolytic anemia would flare, I would call the trainers in the large town two hours away from our small town to schedule a transfusion of two to four units of blood, as needed based on the weekly blood tests I received at the hospital in our small town. When I developed oozing sores on my legs (initially from chigger bites, we supposed.) the acupuncturist suggested I not take the drugs prescribed, just increase the herbs and sessions with him. When two months later, the sores became even more angry and oozing, he suggested I visit a dermatologist.

Not trusting references from any of the before-mentioned health service providers, I decided to travel the two and a half hours to our former large city of residence, to visit my preferred dermatologist friend. She gave me very painful shots into the sores on my ankles and suggested a possible diagnosis. When improvement didn't happen and a lymph node popped through the skin of my thigh as an open and painful wound, she questioned her diagnosis and suggested a visit to my former trainer. Not totally thrilled to go back to my trainer's office, I prayed and decided that no matter what, going to see him would get me connected with the ultimate infectious disease doc, an ongoing hero in my Hilda storyline So, I called my former oncologist's office, and he got me right in, and then directly into the large hospital in my former large city of residence with the ultimate infectious disease doc directing my path toward healing. "Thank you, God!" Maggie and I spontaneously chorus in unison.

After a long period of hospitalization, an even longer duration of intravenous antibiotic treatment, and wound dressage for the big hole in my left thigh, I began a new adventure with Hilda where even Maggie couldn't begin to pretend it was anything like a new normal. Any attempt to subdue Hilda created autoimmune reactions in me, ranging from horrendous and physically transformative sinus infections, weird rashes, fevers, the ever-constant need for hemoglobin and IVIG, a growing wart colony in strategically embarrassing places on my person, and a persistent need for numerous infused antibiotics for the ever-present bacterial and viral infections my tired little body seemed to constantly invite for extended visits.

My trainer could only come up with treatments that created greater complications and more extensive responses of misery and pain. No therapy seemed to work at all anymore. "It's time for a new plan!" Carol Margaret lectured with an exasperated gleam in her eyes. Maggie and I nodded, desperately looking for inspiration, hope, and a vision for healing. Hilda, oblivious to our upheaval, watched our soap opera from the center of the room, all of her elephant sounds, smells, and presence coloring our space with no room for the stirrings of grace, which was probably hiding in the closet to be embraced at the perfect time in our discovery adventure. Our awareness did not include opening the door to that immense gift at this time. We were totally into, "What are we going to *do*?"

It was time to review our options. In my regular visit to my oncologist, I approached the idea of a bone marrow transplant. I explained that the treatments we were undergoing created more problems than solutions. I asked him about options. Nothing he offered me seemed to fit the bill for healing. I asked for a referral to what I later called my favorite transplant docs. My trainer demurred. I asked again. He left the room, and when he returned, he said he would make the call.

When I returned home that day, I could open that closet door. Grace, possibility, and a whole lot of trepidation came pouring out, flooding the house. Maggie, Carol Margaret, and I circled Hilda's commanding presence in the middle of the living room. We joined our hands, raised them high, and with gratitude, Carol Margaret joyfully exclaimed: "We have a plan!"

CHAPTER 10

Falling Down to Get Up

Our first appointment with (whom I soon would affectionately address as) my favorite transplant docs took place in late winter. Their offices were housed in a charming, old hospital that was filled with friendly, caring people and large rooms with beautiful views. To increase my delight, the charming old hospital was named after one of my favorite Christian saints. The charming, old hospital was on the south side of our former large city, so driving from our small town to the south side of our former large city was a trek that often necessitated overnight stays at a hotel in our former large city and the need to board the growing into middle-aged two Labrador retrievers and the increasingly diva-like younger inherited cat at a kennel in our small town.

Our first appointment with one of four favorite transplant docs, the one I grew to think of as Dr. Feel Good, took place on a sunny day in the middle of the morning. The favorite transplant docs had reviewed my records and statistics, etc., and as One Husband and

I alternated glances at Dr. Feel Good and prolonged gazes past the leafless tree line outside the large room's window, Dr. Feel Good shared his recommendations for Hilda's removal, and everything that was involved with the shrinkage of her presence from my person. He even recorded our conversation so we could review all the information and ask even more questions before choosing to buy a ticket for the elephant truck. It seemed every kind of whelming and surreal that we'd come to this crossroad in our Hilda story. A transplant appeared to be our only option medically, and if we didn't get onboard, perhaps there wouldn't be any other mode for our questions to travel into anything other than nothing. "Nothing ventured, nothing gained!" Carol Margaret loves to show off her quotability talents.

One Husband and I felt teary and a bit shell shocked as we drove back to our hotel. We reviewed the information we received, listened to the recording Dr. Feel Good had made from our conversation that morning, and then sought to find varied ways to distract ourselves from the looming deadline of decision making. *Whenever I'm at choice about things, I feel spacious, gracious, and possible,* I thought. ("The world's your oyster!" Maggie emotes.) I've often felt that once the decision is made, my options are defined until the next choice point, and honestly, I can't guarantee I'm always aware enough to recognize that moment. The idea of a transplant inspired Maggie's feeble attempt at creative rhyming humor:

> "Here's your box,
> Jump inside,
> Let us take you for a ride.
> Come on, let's go,
> *Andiamo,*

Healing's way is ever wide.
Hurry now, no time to hide."

I stopped Maggie abruptly and absolutely. What I didn't need in that moment was her dorky humor attempt. "Laughter brings Zen to all experience. Just try it …" Carol Margaret and Maggie smiled compassionately at my anguished dismay. It's so much more than bad poetry … One Husband pats me on the back with empathy for my chagrin. "It always gets better!" he reminds me.

We talked about our options with each other, One Husband and me. Both our lives—physically, mentally, emotionally, and spiritually—would be forever changed by choosing this road to travel. We would need to leave our little cottage in the small town and farm out our middle-aged and charming Labrador retrievers and diva-like, taunting younger inherited cat to unsuspecting relatives for at least several months or even longer. One Husband or some other responsible family member (enter my Super Sister) would need to be with me 24–7 to care for me when I couldn't, and there were numerous accommodations to be made for housing, lifestyle, work, diet, treatment, preparations for treatment—everything that composed our day-to-day living for an indeterminate to forever amount of time, energy, and space. All would be in flux, with no guarantees that anything would be healed, improved, or normal. ("Whatever normal is!" Carol Margaret's eyes roll.) Idina Menzel's soulful rendition of "Brave" was played on repeat as I walked around the lake by our hotel, in shock and seeking solace in prayer, her song, and the honking geese inhabiting the grounds surrounding my sorrow.

After prayer, hugs, tears, walks, and conversation, One Husband and I were ready to say yes to this opportunity for healing. We went to our favorite transplant center in the old and charming hospital with large rooms having beautiful views and friendly, caring people. My port was accessed many times for blood tests—tests to determine compatibility with a donor on the bone marrow registry, tests to determine so many different kinds of information and measurements for which I had no iota of comprehension or understanding of the whys. My favorite transplant docs eased my pressingly worried desires to understand everything by suggesting that I knew more about Hilda than most trainers around; however, what I didn't know, they did. The manner in which they relayed that message still encouraged my questions and desire to know; however, it also increased my ability to extend my trust because they were truly on my team. Super Sister had been tested as a potential donor many years ago, and despite being a good sister, was not a good donor for me. On the registry, not a single person was an exact match. "Celebrate uniqueness." Maggie exuded positivity.

There were two "good matches"/potential donors—not exact matches, but closer than anything else; however one had removed his/her name from the list for a year. My hopes hinged on the health of the one remaining donor and whether he/ she could and would choose to donate her/his stem cells to me.

Meanwhile, while all this testing was done, my trainer and favorite transplant docs thought it might be a good idea if I were the lucky recipient of shots in my belly for twelve weeks, three times a week to help curb the extreme amount of elephantitis I was experiencing.

They and we believed that it might be easier for the transplant to work if Hilda were a bit less prevalent in my blood and bone marrow. So while we were testing and waiting for results from testing, I commuted to the hotel in our former large city from our small-town cottage, leaving the animals with One Husband to go to my trainer's office three times a week for a single shot in my belly. While at the hotel, I worked on getting strong for the transplant, eating well, gaining weight, walking miles and miles and miles daily, journaling, visiting with friends, savoring the aliveness of being back in my former large city, missing our now-rented home filled with a family who, we learned, had no intention of buying or maintaining our home like it was their own. Maggie encouraged me to find the gift in the fact that they paid rent so that we weren't bankrupt. I whispered, "Thank you ... maybe?"

After six weeks of spending all but the weekends apart from One Husband, our middle-aged, charming Labrador retrievers, and an increasingly hissy diva-like inherited cat, my favorite transplant docs suggested we do a bone marrow biopsy to determine if the shots were making a difference. The results of the biopsy showed the shots had not worked to decrease the density of the CLL and that, in fact, there was a chromosome abnormality that had developed, prompting me to become chemo-resistant. Without a transplant, I was told I could have three to six months to live.

What I started to believe and truly grew to acknowledge and appreciate in this part of my healing adventure became what I embraced more assuredly in the coming days, months, and years: my experience taught me that all general prognosis, even diagnosis, is artful, educated conjecture. Anything is possible. Miracles are always available to one who visions, dreams, accepts, and transforms. Open heart, open mind, personal responsibility, prayer, and thanksgiving.

So … one reliably educated authority predicted three to six mon[—]
No one knew. Verses of scripture, of hope, possibility, and, grace
flooded my mind. "This moment is the only moment, and in this
moment, all things are possible!" Maggie expressed our position.
Thank you, Maggie.

I went to my trainer's office and told him the results of the biopsy.
I'm not certain he heard what I said when he suggested I continue
with the shots, just in case. I repeated my biopsy results (which he
had already received, but not reviewed) and my decision to cease
poking my growing almost abundant belly (walking and eating had
graced me with tummy padding for a transplant) with needles full of
chemicals. My trainer suggested that our separation would not be for
long. I could come back and be his patient after my transplant! *No
way, Jose*, I thought. I did not experience hopeful aspiration in our
last meeting together. Going into a grand adventure like an elephant
transplant and hearing my oncologist promote eternal patient hood
with him as my go-to doc, a permanent "just in case" physician, was
hardly a message I wanted to accept or allow in my sphere of vision
or reference. Thankfully, my favorite transplant docs told me they'd
always be there for me, forever. They shared with me that, even when
I was well, I would always be welcome for hellos, smiles, and hugs!
"Our kind of doctoring," we said, grinning affirmatively.

The favorite transplant docs had decided I would receive a pre-
transplant conditioning treatment of total body irradiation and
chemotherapy the week before the stem cells would be infused into
my body. They told me I would need a triple lumen catheter inserted
in my chest. I thought to myself how conveniently prepared I would
be for infusions, transfusions, blood draws, and flushes with my port
and the triple lumen catheter.

· the transplant. One Husband and I made
· the animals. Super Sister took one especially
ed Labrador retriever and the hissy diva-like
y she earned her title "Super" sister?). Elder
successful Son relocated to become a homeowner in our former
large city. He was happy to be responsible and loving to the other
wonderfully charming, middle-aged Labrador retriever. Loving care
for the animals was handled, and we made plans for our annual
family reunion to be held at Super Sister's home far away from our
small town and former large city. We planned to gather as a family
for our reunion as we transported animals to her care until we were
able to retrieve them home.

Elder Son's middle-aged and wonderfully charming Labrador
retriever was originally one of his favorite Christmas gifts, so we
would only get to visit and babysit this canine, but he lived in our
former large city, and I felt hopeful we could visit often. Younger,
excelling in graduate school, Son lived close to Super Sister, so I
would get to see him at the reunion and hopefully, over the holidays
that year. We planned the reunion/animal exchange for a couple
weeks before the scheduled transplant.

The next step was getting a place to live during the first two or more
months of the transplant experience. Our favorite transplant docs
suggested we begin this process as an outpatient, although I would
probably require hospitalization at some point during my treatment.
They asked that we find a place to stay close to the charming old
Christian saint hospital with friendly, caring people and large rooms
with beautiful views. Fortunately, the favorite transplant docs had
a connection with a housing development a couple blocks from the
hospital. We were thrilled. Our plans were unfolding smoothly.

And then … a potential glitch. Apparently the donor to whom my blood matched had problems with his/her blood, and the transplant would need to be delayed as the donor received treatment for what obstacle could prevent her/him from donating stem cells. Not choosing to allow ourselves to get discouraged, we drove to Super Sister's for an awesome reunion and a tearful good-bye, particularly to the especially charming, middle-aged Labrador retriever now in her loving care. One Husband and I journeyed somberly back to our tiny, quiet cottage in our small town to wait and wonder.

How grateful I was for One Husband's loyal care and loving attention! In those days of waiting and wondering, he became Number One Husband—the guy I'd always loved and always would—and I grew to recognize how much I would get to be opened, nakedly vulnerable, and necessarily dependent on him as we foraged to find our way on this journey. That particular mode of being was uncomfortable for me and would require more courage and trust than I'd ever brought to our relationship in the twenty-nine years we had been married. It required sacrifice from him, major changes in how we usually operated, and our level of intimacy transformed into more than we had allowed or expressed before this time of unknowing. In spite of all the uncertainties, I experienced so much love, so much joy, and so many blessings—all inspiring heights of inexpressible gratitude, overflowing with such powerful flow that I knew that, no matter what, all is well, and all would be well. Thank you, Julian of Norwich.

We waited together. We shared our fears, our thoughts, and our feelings. We walked into the unknown as a team, and it changed our partnership forever. During the unknown and dark places, our marriage transformed into something larger than it had been. Thank you, Hilda. Thank you, God.

Finally, we received a call from our favorite transplant docs. My donor had overcome whatever obstacle would preclude donation of stem cells. We were given a date for the infusion and instructions to come to the small town south of our former large city within a few short weeks. The impending reality of what was about to occur was upon us.

Number One Husband helped me cut my hair incredibly short to curb the shedding into baldness that would inevitably occur with the prescribed pre-treatment, conditioning regimen. We packed suitcases and read voraciously about possibilities for our transplant adventure, until we could no longer absorb another nugget or analyze any implied nuance. "Just take it as it comes. Stay in the here and now," Maggie advised us.

One of the favorite activities I loved in anticipation of the transplant was listening to music. Music brings all "once upon a times" into my heart as the presence of the present and was the quickest transport to heart-centered living for most of my holy life. Choosing to create a playlist of music for inspiration and encouragement during this adventure, I consciously picked and channeled songs that reflected my desired vision of healing. An eclectic list of songs, I copied it onto discs for my family and closest friends. I called it "Maggie/Mom's Transplant Mix." When those family members and friends asked how they could support me, I suggested listening to this CD as a prayer for me because its music sang my soul song.

"My healing is everyone's healing." Maggie and I nodded our heads in agreement as we smiled our intentions, singing the songs of our heart.

We made arrangements to stay at a hotel in our former large town until our apartment, near the charming old hospital with friendly, caring people, large rooms with beautiful views, named after one of my favorite Christian saints, would be available. We loaded up the car with everything we thought we might need or want for the next possibly several months. We said farewell to friends and neighbors in our small town, no clarity around if or when I'd see them again. A kind neighbor made me a beautiful fleece blanket. It was assorted colors on one side, and the material on the other side was colored a deep blue, reflecting the lake outside our cottage. She reminded me to remember the lake reflecting the peace, joy, and beautiful view from the windows of our home. I thought, *I can pretend I'm by the lake when things get unbearable.* With tears in my eyes and a lump in my throat, I said thank you, and we closed the car doors. Hilda blubberingly heaved herself onto the trunk with a less-than-gracious, bellowing kerplunk, and we drove our fully loaded vehicle down the road for our auspicious date with destiny.

CHAPTER 11

Going Down to Be, Do, Have It All

(a.k.a., "Getting Down" to Living from Vision and Intention)

Waiting and Wondering

It was a sunny Monday morning in mid-August when we arrived at a brother hospital with the same name as the charming old hospital named after one of my favorite Christian saints, with large rooms, beautiful views, and friendly, caring people. This hospital was newer, bigger, and located north of the charming old hospital, at the southern edge of our former large city. We found a parking spot close to the numbered entrance in which we were directed to enter the facility. Grudgingly and sluggishly, Hilda tailed Number One Husband and me through the door to the newer, bigger, named after the same favorite saint hospital. We were here to be measured for the container I would occupy during my total body irradiation.

Number One Husband kissed me good-bye as he prepared himself to comfortably wait, drink coffee, and read/work in the waiting/wondering room—a routine he would perfect with extensive practice during this transplant adventure. Hilda and I were directed to a cold, large room with what looked like a cardboard container on a stage with a white wall as a backdrop. ("Oh my! It looks like a coffin!" Carol Margaret covered her open mouth with horror.) A large, arc-shaped disc dominated the main floor of the room. I was instructed to get in the box, curl up in fetal position, and remain absolutely still while the technicians constructed what appeared to be Styrofoam pieces to mold around me. The technician told me I could bring favorite music for my listening pleasure. Luckily, I had a disc in my purse of my favorite transplant mix, and I gave it to her. Although I had plans to bring her all of my favorites for the joy of variety, she played that same cd throughout my radiation treatments, twice a day for four days, an hour and a half to almost three hours each time. That music became engraved upon my experience. "I wonder if all the other people in the room were sick and tired of hearing it." Carol Margaret gets kind of snarly sometimes.

So, after we were fitted for our "coffin," we were released to Number One Husband in the waiting/wondering room with instructions to return the next day to begin our four-day process of this method of preparing for Hilda's exit and my advent of life without her. Number One Husband drove us to the small town south of our former large city to the charming old hospital with friendly, caring people, large rooms with beautiful views, and the offices of my favorite transplant docs, named after one of my favorite Christian saints. I would get to be weighed, measured, and assessed, have blood taken, and meet with the on-call favorite transplant doc, a new daily event in the life of patient undergoing elephant release (a.k.a., stem cell transplant).

All of my favorite transplant docs were very involved with my care, and all of them had nicknames they or others had gifted them. Dr. Feel Good (the name says it all) was my primary doctor. The others included Dr. Chalkboard (a gifted teacher and wonderful at explaining everything with visual graphics), Dr. Dutch (great accent and entertaining stories), and Dr. Gloom and Doom (a true misnomer because, although this doc always told it like he saw it, he did everything with honesty, compassion, dedication, deliberation, humility, authenticity, and sincerity … "Amen!" Maggie stops my exaltation with her exclamation.) We were so thankful for all of our favorite transplant docs. The nurses were fantastic caregivers, and Number One Husband always received great attention with his waiting/wondering room trademark cup of coffee. "Truly service with a smile," Maggie says, winking. We felt good about everything and everybody as we worked our way through day 1 of transplant preparation.

After our check-in with our favorite transplant docs and company, we worked our way to the surgical area of the charming old hospital, and Number One Husband got to discover another waiting and wondering room. I followed a nurse back to a dressing room and prepared for surgery to implant my triple lumen catheter. The procedure itself was a blur, but when I emerged from the basement of the charming old hospital's recovery room, a huge appendage was imbedded on the opposite side of my chest as my port. "No more tight tops. No way to hide this contraption." Carol Margaret shook her head as she planned our wardrobe.

We left the hospital late afternoon and ran errands, went out to dinner, and then went to our hotel in our former large city. Our apartment close to the charming old hospital would not be available until sometime the next day. The next day we would go morning and afternoon to the newer, bigger hospital on the south side of our former large city, with visits to the favorite transplant docs and a move in to the apartment we would call home for the next few months somewhere on the schedule.

The days went smoothly as planned. We both waited and wondered if all this was working. What should we be feeling? We didn't know; we just were in this space and following the program. One day melded into another. By the weekend the total body irradiation was finished, and none too soon for a cramped-up Carol. "At least you know you don't want to spend eternity in a pine box! Cremation might be your experience based choice?" Maggie is always dying to find the gift in everything!

Chemotherapy, at the old, charming hospital with friendly, caring people, large rooms with beautiful views, named after one of my favorite Christian saints in the offices of my favorite transplant docs, was administered by one of my favorite transplant nurses all weekend to further subdue Hilda. Hilda was getting really quiet and sleepy, out of it, whatever "it" was. One of my favorite transplant nurses and I talked about God, life, love, and family and the time flew as I was infused and flushed, and Number One Husband continued with his preferred waiting/wondering ritualized routine.

Finally, it was transplant day! I wondered when the stem cells would arrive and what it would be like receiving them. As we wondered, we continued to wait. The transplant docs said they were unsure of when packed cells would arrive by special courier.

They also suggested the blood might need to be thinned or strained before I received it. We waited in our apartment for the call to go get on the elephant truck and say good-bye to Hilda and hello to a brand-new immune system. I wondered where my donor was from, who my donor was … I imagined all kinds of things, which was the way I spent time huddled under my blue blanket, feeling the lethargic effects of pretreatment, waiting and wondering—the predominant theme of this chapter of our adventure.

We drove to the charming old hospital for our daily weigh-in and blood test and flushes. We were told once again that we would be called when the cells arrived. It was after 8:00 p.m. when we received a call to come to the favorite transplant docs' offices in the charming old hospital. Armed with my fleece blanket, transplant mix music, Number One Husband, bottled water, and a very weak and droopy Hilda, we arrived to a large room with a dark but beautiful view, friendly, caring people, favorite transplant nurses, and Dr. Gloom and Doom, who was working on the stem cells to prepare them for me. Number One Husband waited and wondered from his corner of the room, and I listened to my transplant mix on the bed, as Maggie led us in prayer. We were mastering this wait and wonder thing, I assured myself.

Finally, the courier, another favorite transplant employee, arrived with a cooler containing the stem cells. I assumed we would get started immediately, but she delayed the process as she told me that first I must open the sealed envelope she gingerly handed me. Really wondering at this point, I grasped the envelope, tore it open, and saw a card inside with a note from my donor. Donor told me he/she was praying for me, included prayers and well wishes from a prayer group she/he was a part of, and also included in his/her card one of my favorite old testament scripture verses, Jeremiah 29:11: "For surely I know the plans I have for you, says the Lord, plans for your welfare and not for harm, to give you a future with hope." It was a touching and tearful moment. Maggie started humming, "Surely the presence of the Lord is in this place," and my heart welled with an enormous, "Thank you, God!"

I received the stem cells, my heart overflowing with thanksgiving and joy that, because of a beloved stranger somewhere in the world saying yes to donating stem cells, I was gifted an opportunity for a rebirth of health, life, and possibility. I could see Hilda drooling in the dark corner by the window.

We returned to the apartment—couldn't quite call it "home" yet—after 11:00 p.m., and as I laid awake in bed, I felt overcome with gratitude and gracious, hopeful wonderfulness. I could hardly contain my awe at what was happening. Another and an always— thank you, God!

Number One Husband organized all the medications I got to take to augment this adventure in a very large pillbox with barely enough room for the number of pills my favorite transplant docs prescribed for me. I was lucky enough to take these assorted pills morning, noon, and night, and because I was feeling a little puny and maybe starting to spike a little fever, I felt so grateful Number One Husband was in charge. He also became responsible for all cooking, cleaning, laundry, driving—you name it, he did it. Every day we trekked over to the charming old hospital two blocks away for blood work, vitals, flushes, and weigh in. Most of the time I huddled under my blanket, fitfully sleeping and doing whatever Number One Husband told me to do.

When my fevers became more prevalent, I was admitted as an inpatient to the transplant wing of the charming old hospital with friendly, caring people, large rooms with beautiful views, named after one of my favorite Christian saints. My favorite transplant docs gave me more medications, and some of them made me feel a bit (actually much more than a bit) loopy, and I don't remember very much of my first two-week stint in the transplant wing (the "Dark Side," Dr. Feel Good calls it). It was entirely a blur. I remember Super Sister came to visit. The blinds were closed so I couldn't admire the beautiful views, people wore masks when they visited, and my skin began to itch, hurt, and shed, just like a snake. Dr. Chalkboard shared clearly about ten-day syndrome and graft versus host disease (another actively prevalent, non-easeful state of body, mind, spirit), so it kind of made sense when I was coherent, a rarity at this point in my experience. Good thing about Super Sister and Number One Husband—they witnessed, heard, and relayed what I couldn't process at the time, and I felt very grateful.

Elder Son and his Great Girlfriend came to visit and brought me artificial roses that looked real and a jersey of my favorite football player. Fabulous friends stopped by briefly with well wishes and love. I was glad I was well enough to interact consciously with them, but I didn't get to hug them. I didn't like being out of it. Super Sister told me I wasn't out of it when people I knew—nurses, friends, family—came to the room, only when they left. (Guess my performing background paid dividends with the "rising to the occasion" thing.)

I was released on a Sunday, in time for the first home football game for our former large city's favored football team. I left the hospital wearing the jersey of my favorite football player, carrying my big blue blanket, and hopeful I'd seen the last of the "Dark Side." Going back to the apartment truly felt like going home, at least this time!

Actually, I was beginning to feel numb with this stuff. It had been less than a month since I received Donor's cells, and side effects were numerous. While I was in the transplant wing of the charming old hospital, the rest of my hair was falling out in clumps, so Number One Husband shaved my head over a wastebasket. I had all kinds of allergies to antibiotics, so the infectious disease docs (an efficient group that served this charming old hospital) desensitized my body to a drug they felt I needed to take daily during this adventure. This process included being awakened every half hour all night long to take this foul-tasting drug in incremental amounts so my body could tolerate it enough for me to take it on a daily basis for the next year or so. All I can say upon reflection is, I did it. Every day I was required to shower with an antibacterial wash, and although I love to be clean, it was not fun or pretty. My body was chilled, skin shedding, and I felt weak and nauseous. Diarrhea was constant, and I started to lose weight because I had little appetite. With my loose clothing, you couldn't really tell, because I was developing the infamous prednisone moon face, something I couldn't even notice because I couldn't see myself clearly in the mirror.

It had become a time of perseverance and endurance with bits of humor interjected via Number One Husband and his daily Tiger Woods golf video game, a fun phone conversation or visit with Super Sister, bad jokes from Dr. Feel Good, or calls from Elder Son and Younger Son. I did not sleep very well, and as I look back on this time, I realize all these complaints and issues are irrelevant. I did what I did to get through obstacles, hard times, and discomfort because my focus was on the vision—in this case, wellness was the prize, and going through this experience I chose to bring whatever it takes to get there, unattached to what it looked like. I knew with every fiber of my being that no matter what, everything always gets better. I often detached and stopped feeling my pain—except when I didn't. I tried to journal, and I prayed when I could. The weird thing is I love to pray. It's the joy of my life; except during this experience, very often, I couldn't. It was a time when one day flowed into the next and into another until months had gone by, and all of life revolved around treatment, medication, doc visits, tests, weigh-ins, flushes, measurements, biopsies. Number One Husband and I had no other life than the day-to-day management of graft versus host disease, symptoms and side effects of drugs, rule following, attention to new issues, talking about bathroom habits, and what to eat for dinner that wasn't fresh food or germy, but would appeal to a picky eater (me) who preferred organic, fresh, and raw—all *verboten* during this stage of the transplant adventure. The ultimate question loomed, "Was this whole thing working?" Although unspoken, the question permeated our every experience.

When we approached the six-week mark post-transplant, we received permission to visit our cottage on the lake in the small town where we had lived before the transplant. It was as if we'd been given wings—very freeing to get away for an overnight. It felt so energizing to me, and Maggie and I danced around the cottage with joy before I retreated to my chair to rest and revere the view.

When Super Sister came to visit (she came to visit every month that year), we went to visit Elder Son and the wonderfully charming middle-aged Labrador retriever who lived with him. Life had moments of uplifting connections, and I looked forward to those lift-gifts with great anticipation.

At the end of two months, we were more than ready to move out of our apartment close to the charming old hospital. It had served its purpose, and we were grateful, but it wasn't home. We were able to really go home to our cottage in the small town with the caveat that we come south for regularly scheduled visits, initially three times a week. We were cautioned to be aware of a whole very long list of "call the doc" items. I don't actually recall how events unfolded during this time. Maggie tells me I have a gift of forgetting the stuff that makes me uncomfortable. We had a great relationship with the hotel we frequented in our former large city so I kept a "just in case" room reserved there, where I kept clothes, supplies, etc., for the frequent times we needed to stay overnight with our doctoring or the impromptu hospital admission.

The worst effect of the entire experience was graft versus host disease. All kinds of surprises blessed my person with this attack of donor cells versus leukemia cells. Supposedly this GVHD was very good for getting Hilda out of my body. She was rather stubborn and resistant, so all this invasive stuff was good at beating her out of her hiding place under the bed. Another interesting piece of information I learned was that with the induction of my donor's cells and a new immune system, I also inherited a new blood type. Whereas I used to be O negative ("The universal donor who could never give blood ..." Maggie knows my litany), I was now an A positive ("An A+!" Carol Margaret, overachiever that she is, proudly announces our grade with a big smile). So many complex, amazing, and miraculous changes happening in my little body—I could hardly grasp all the significance of each happening. Luckily, my favorite transplant docs did. They were on top of everything before I could surmise a problem.

Donor was a regular at sending notes with scripture, holiday cards, and well wishes. I often wondered how Donor knew so many of my favorite verses. "It's a God thing," Maggie insisted. I tended to agree and loved living with such awe and wonder. I couldn't communicate with Donor until a year after transplant, but I could send Donor anonymous letters/gifts that would be scrutinized by the Bone Marrow Registry people to make certain no identities were inadvertently disclosed. I decided to create a CD of songs expressing how I felt about the donor's contribution to my life. I figured words couldn't express what music could, and if the music were insufficient at best, at least I had prayer and could thank God for the donor. It is very odd writing a letter addressed, "Dear Donor," and signing it, "Your Stem Cell Recipient." Something was kind of missing with this type of communication, but it was the best we had going so I wasn't going to complain more than I did. I also mailed Donor a favorite bracelet (knowing how Donor loved scripture) engraved "With God, all things are possible." I often thought about whether I wanted to know who Donor really was when that choice became available. Maggie advised me to cross that bridge when I got there. I took a deep breath and nodded my agreement. Another wonder and wait …

We wondered if the transplant were working. There were different tests to measure different stuff that I barely recall now. At the time it felt like everything required more waiting and wondering, until that whole way of operating became second nature. Maggie suggested that patience and living the questions were the modalities creating miraculous possibility, and that we would be wise to adopt them as permanent habits. I decided I'd take my time and wonder about that idea …

Down Deep and Desperate

There was a special and very expensive (thank you, medical insurance!) blood test that measured how much of me was Carol Margaret Hohlfelder Roth and how much of me was donor. The goal was to be 100 percent donor, although at the core of me I questioned, "What happens to Carol Margaret Hohlfelder Roth? Where does she go?" Carol Margaret rolled her eyes at my pondering and suggested I expand my paradigm to embrace the broadness of my possible extension of being. "Live the '*and*,'" she chastised. Maggie looked blank and befuddled, and I felt like throwing up my arms and giving up all mental machinations in my futility of understanding. "Go with the flow. Just be here now," Maggie encouraged me.

This "who's who" test was performed fairly often, and the desired goal was total conquest and victory for Donor and the absolute banishment of Hilda. Hilda, however, was very loyal and committed to recalcitrance, so this was something like a knockdown, punch-in-the-gut, drag-out tournament of immune systems, persons, and medicines, a Donor versus Hilda fight, and it was rather challenging to place odds on a sure winner with this battle. Who was favored, Hilda or Donor? Now it truly was wait, wonder, and watch. My graft versus host disease was watched, and treatment was tweaked according to what was evidenced with tests, exams, and experience. Some of the GVHD was desirable because it delivered a knockdown punch in the gut to Hilda, but too much took the tipping point to pain, despair, illness, suffering, and an enigma for me (whoever "I" was at this point in our adventure). I loved the way my favorite transplant docs explained this situation, especially Dr. Dutch with his colorful storytelling. All my favorite transplant docs considered their approach to healing an art, rather than a science. We smiled in assent and imagined broad and beautiful strokes of paint on a canvas.

As fall approached winter, I had not seen much change in my status, and the GVHD required massive doses of steroids, especially prednisone, the drug with which I'd shared a love/hate relationship the entire time Hilda lived with me. Sometimes I would get to travel to the charming old hospital to get infusions of steroids to arrest the fever or the other varied strategies Hilda utilized to fight the donor. My skin continued to shed, my fingernails and toenails fell off, and my hairless condition, especially my bald as a ping pong ball head, which topped a very large full moon face with dry red and yellow eyes, prompted me to avoid mirrors and public appearances, where well-meaning persons often addressed me as Number One Husband's aged mother or Super Sister's feeble mother or aunt (because, in my best moments, we'd always resembled each other in appearance), or nieces' and nephews' sickly grandmother.

We discovered mid-autumn that Elder Son's wonderfully charming middle-aged Labrador retriever was diagnosed with a cancer called osteosarcoma. There was little to be done except for pain management. Because Elder Son's home contained many flights of stairs and wonderfully charming middle-aged Labrador retriever needed to be carried to get anywhere, Number One Husband and I took him back to the cottage in our small town, a home with just a few stairs, an amount Number One Husband could handle carrying a ninety-pound dog. At Christmastime, we planned to drive to Super Sister's home to celebrate as a family and bring home especially charming middle-aged Labrador retriever. (Number One Husband was not a fan of the diva-like hissy inherited cat, to my chagrin. Super Sister loved her and agreed to keep the diva-like hissy inherited cat. Number One Husband did the closest thing he had ever attempted to resembling a happy dance!) Our goal was to keep Elder Son's wonderfully charming middle-aged Labrador retriever comfortable and alive until wonderfully charming middle-aged Labrador retriever could be together again with especially charming middle-aged Labrador retriever because they were forever siblings. Christmas was wonderful, and we returned home to reunite the charming, middle-aged Labrador retrievers. The wonderfully charming middle-aged Labrador retriever died a few weeks later, and Number One Husband and I became responsible parents again to an especially charming middle-aged, this time solo, Labrador retriever ("Have compassion for your reader and call the canine Brown Dog, please." Carol Margaret loves to tell me what to do.) Officially we became a threesome, and Brown Dog went everywhere we went and gave us something outside of worry, waiting, watching, and wondering. Love and joy were the gifts of this aging puppy, and we were grateful to be together again.

As winter that year came into full expression, so did Hilda. It appeared we would need more than graft versus host disease to increase the donor's odds. Weekly chemotherapy was advised, as well as a process called photopherisis. Photopherisis involved lying in a bed attached to a machine where blood was removed from my body, exposed to ultraviolet light, and then returned to my body. It was supposed to help with graft versus host disease. It took varying amounts of time, depending on how quickly my blood flowed. We loved our favorite transplant photopherisis nurse and enjoyed great conversation, and care so time went quickly. Over the course of treatment, for about a year, sometimes as often as three times a week, we spent much time together. Very grateful I am for such great nursing and friendship. Oftentimes I received chemotherapy as I was doing photopherisis. ("I love to multitask, don't you?" Maggie loves making everything a positive.)

That winter there was a hospitalization or two, and I lost a considerable amount of weight. The chemo lowered my blood counts, low enough that the favorite transplant docs took away one of my chemical cocktails. By the time spring approached, an MRI showed the majority of the discs in my back were bulging or herniated. ("Who cares what they were labeled? They hurt," Carol Margaret snips.) I was in enough pain with my joints, muscles, bones, whole body that I actually took potent prescribed painkillers, curled up in a ball on the bed under a blanket, and allowed myself to do and feel even less than nothing. I had never experienced anything like this pain in my life, so I disappeared, literally, figuratively, and any other way I could imagine. All I could do was keep telling myself that it always gets better. This particularly horrible part of my adventure—it, too, would pass. Thank you, God.

At this point in my treatment process, we spent the majority of our time at the hotel in our former large city (with occasional trips to our cottage or to the "Dark Side" for a few days to treat a side effect or infection), keeping us close to the charming old hospital. Brown Dog would go with us to treatment at the charming old hospital in the small town south of our former large city because he loudly voiced his displeasure when he remained without us at the hotel (a.k.a., frenetic barking). Number One Husband changed his waiting and wondering rituals to include walking and watering Brown Dog, and he especially enjoyed the friendly, caring people and the large rooms with beautiful views, which allowed him to excel in his care of especially charming middle-aged solo Labrador retriever (a.k.a., Brown Dog).

Arthritis attacked my joints, and I needed help getting up and down the few steps at our cottage. By the middle of spring that year, Number One Husband took me to the favorite transplant center in the charming old hospital named after one of my favorite Christian saints in a wheelchair because it was too painful for me to walk. At that appointment Dr. Gloom and Doom and I had a conversation I still hold in my heart. With a tear in his eye, he shared with me that the favorite transplant docs were doing everything they could think of and that they had some concerns with their awareness that I wasn't significantly improving. He said that he would let me know if or when they couldn't do anything else. I so appreciated his talking with me the way he did. Thank you, Dr. Gloom and Doom.

Maggie went to prayer, Carol Margaret went to "what ifs" and planning a memorial service, and I just felt detached from all of it. When Super Sister or Number One Husband asked me what I was feeling, the answer was nothing, numb, detached, surrendered, not afraid, and committed to my mantra: it always gets better, no matter what. Actually, I was "in it to win it," whatever it was, not sure how we'd get there. Hilda was attached to me, and her attachment really was killing my aspirations, inspirations, and intentional vision for physical wellness. I was grateful for others' prayers when I couldn't pray, for loving kindness when I couldn't feel (literally and figuratively) and for time (Like the song, "Tomorrow"! Maggie gets inspired and starts singing, "The sun will come up … Only/Always a day away!")

At my absolute low point, I was surprised by Super Sister making an unscheduled visit to the charming old hospital on a day when I was given the joy of arriving for photopheresis and chemotherapy on wheelchair wheels, escorted by Number One Husband. Also in attendance were some of my favorite transplant nurses, and Dr. Feel Good. It was a pivotal day for me that turned into the expression of a miracle. I can't say what stemmed the tide that day, but after that weird day when the entire universe seemed to come together as if conspiring to create a healing vortex, my health began to improve. There were still obstacles, Hilda, treatments, medications, GVHD, and side effects from everything, but possibility became the starring role, and it was front row center. The "edge of beginning again" I could name this day, this feeling of hope. What I do know is that I started experiencing glimpses of me again—growing into the wholeness and the wellness I really and already was. No more desperation or despair—if not evident in my demeanor before this day, it emerged from its buried crevices deep down inside me from unknown depths. This turning point, this incredible crucible empowered me to reach deep down and discard the yuckiness, the doubts, the abandoned pieces of myself that no longer served the newness I was birthing ... Hope reigned from that day on, and it has not faltered since. ("Error ... Except when it has." Carol Margaret corrects my generalization.) No feasible rationalization, justifiable belief, certifiable truth or scientific explanation ... Thank you, miraculous possibility.

Farewell

Every story gets to get where it's going, and this transplant adventure does, too. Hilda moved in with me in 1998 and stuck with me through thick and thin, hot and cold, up and down, in and out, rich and poor, inspired and lost, whole and broken—name the contrasts, and we had been, done, seen, and experienced all of them. There are so many new age thoughts/recommendations/epistles about not naming, accepting, or acknowledging what is not in balance or not in ease within us. Living with an elephant for almost fifteen years was similar to adopting her as family and adapting to what she brought to my life, as I am called to do with a family member. I didn't always like her way of being or her attachment to me, but she and I had chosen each other. Whether I did so in full awareness or not, I was responsible for this elephant, this Hilda, Health Imbalance Leukemia Diagnosis Adventure. I created her, drew her to me, sourced her—deliberately or inadvertently, it really didn't matter. What mattered was my response to this elephant, and with my power of choice I could accept Hilda and choose possible means of releasing her, with love and gratitude for the good she brought to my life.

Yes, I said good, love, and gratitude—all that most of us would not normally associate with a diagnosis of cancer. *And* if I dig through the pile of manure long enough, I can always find a pony, or imagine that I do. Hilda wasn't bad and wrong unless I believed in bad and wrong. Hilda couldn't ruin my life unless I let her. Hilda wouldn't take over my life unless I allowed her to rule my life. Hilda couldn't kill me anymore than crossing the street and being hit by a bus would. As my beloved grandmother from the infamous porch swing used to say, "Well, Carol … Something's got to get us."

Every living thing in physical form is destined to die, to exit a physical housing for heart, mind, and soul. What power we give to ourselves for adventurous living and dying determines whether we find the gifts—the good, the love, and the God in experience. All of what is can take a subjective twist in what we can vision for our lives, our healing, and our fullness of possibility. In our subjective reality, we can recognize who we are in what we see, all we experience, and awaken to the awareness that we can embrace change, tumult, choice, and freedom as the transformative persons we were created to be. Carol Margaret claps enthusiastically at the scholarly expression of what we are discovering to be our more or less justifiable beliefs for our relationship with Hilda and company.

After that magical day when hope dominated our vision, Hilda began to lose her trepidacious dauntingness. The favorite transplant docs kept tweaking treatment, and although improvement was slow, it was happening, and we felt grateful. Number One Husband got back to his regular/pre-transplant work life. I became able to fend for myself, efficiently and sufficiently in numerous, if not all, ways. As spring unfolded, I started walking regularly. The walks were slower and shorter than ever before, but it brought delight, strength, and the sense of accomplishment back to the life of Carol Margaret Hohlfelder Roth. I felt so ambitious I thought to take a walk with Brown Dog. "Bad idea," Carol Margaret muttered as Brown Dog's exuberance promptly pulled us to the ground with a resounding thud and a painful collection of bruises on my backside. Becoming strong enough to walk with Brown Dog became a primary goal, a challenge to master. Maggie and I kiss Brown Dog between the eyes, the special place, Maggie tells me, where, when kissed or softly stroked, animals know they are loved. I decided to celebrate the small things with great love. Thank you, Mother Teresa.

That summer, Elder and Younger Sons came to visit, and we hosted the annual family reunion at our small town cottage. Family stayed close by at a grand hotel, and our annual family talent show was held in a quaint little room at the grand hotel. My hair had begun to grow, and both Number One Husband and Super Sister remarked how much I reminded them of Billy Crystal with my new hairdo. By the end of the summer, the "do" was an uncanny resemblance to Angela Davis. "Quite a variety of talent, humor, and activism represented in one head of hair." Maggie expressed such a musing with a grin as she patted my curly, kinky hair.

Late that summer I was able to drive independently to the charming old hospital each week and stay at the hotel in our former large city. As the first year morphed into the second year, these visits continued. I drove west with Super Sister to visit Elder Nephew and then to our middle-sized hometown. I kept improving, and except for a few hospitalizations and setbacks, everything was getting better and better and better.

Number One Husband suggested we take a vacation to celebrate success. Because of my compromised immune system and germ-infested close-quartered airplanes, we decided to drive to a place that was warm and wonderful and close to Super Sister's home so we could visit her and her family. Before our long drive to this warm, wonderful, close to Super Sister destination, I was treated to another bone marrow biopsy and a "who's who?" test. Dr. Feel Good told me he would call me with the results when they arrived and wished us a happy vacation.

Armed with pillbox, clothes, and accessories for warm weather and wonderful places, we found loving care for Brown Dog while we were away and hopped (figuratively more than literally) into our car for a long drive. I slept fitfully most of the way on the road, called out for more pit and stretch stops than in the past, and felt challenged to sit or sleep anywhere that trip—wonderful places and warm weather included. One day, in the middle of our vacation, Dr. Feel Good

CAROL M. H. ROTH

called with the awesome announcement that I was *all donor*! I had hoped Hilda was missing in action, but I wasn't confident she would ever choose to leave me. I kept thinking I'd find her in a closet, in a suitcase, or under the bed when I least suspected to discover her. I had said good-bye to her too many times to count. Could this be truly the real good-bye, the final farewell?

Number One Husband and I did our happy dance. (We were getting to be quite the practiced happy dancers, and I think Number One Husband was starting to like it.) We called Elder Son, Younger Son, and Super Sister to share our gleeful news. I'm not certain, but Maggie imagined all of them were joyfully happy dancing, too. ("Probably an expressed modification of their genetic gift from earthly father's mother, Grandma Cha-Cha," Carol Margaret figures as she rock steps. "Cha, cha cha.") We move in unison. Thank you, Grandma Cha-Cha!

After sharing the good health news with my family and friends, I reviewed my next steps. Hilda had left me. Was it a permanent departure? She had taken her own sweet time to go—fourteen years or more. Why did I still take all these drugs? How could I become medicine free and keep her away from me? Carol Margaret's research and planning mode of operation went into overdrive.

For our farewell to be permanent ... was that even a possibility? Enter subjective thinking, an intentional vision for my life, living causally, unfolding the questions, imagining the possibilities, learning the responsibilities ... all these growths in awareness of grace, goodness, and love, that came from living with Hilda for so long. The next steps into awareness become unfolding the questions involved with reinvention of my life without Hilda. It was time to get down to exploring and exploiting the "goods" of the adventure and tying them into the next blanket of this story.

When I say "goods," my expression emanates from a belief I hold to be true for me: All is good. All is God. All is love. Distortions of this truth that I hold dear create the pain, havoc, suffering, chaos, evil, and fear experienced in my world. My vision for the world is where good, peace, and love are intended by all people. (Maggie nudges me to change all people to all creation, a reflection of her refusal to accept limited imagining. "That includes Hilda!" Carol Margaret self-righteously loves to have the last word with everything.) If everyone would choose to imagine world of good, love, peace, and God ... Maggie interrupts me singing "Imagine." Thank you, John Lennon.

The Goods

INTRODUCTION

So many "goods" inspired me at the announcement of Hilda's exit.
At first I was giddy, then disbelieving. Amazed, thankful, and then,
fearful. What if she wasn't really gone? What if she came back?
What would life be like without her? Where was the award-winning
marching band, the fantastically orchestrated fanfare in my honor,
the solemn good-bye ceremony with medals, engraved monuments,
and applause, a significant transformational and radical change in
my physical person? It was good news, I was happy—which was
good—and I must have been a good girl/patient/student to have
created the means for this miracle to have evidenced itself in my
life. What could I do with all this goodness? Maggie suggested we
focus on releasing the fear piece because love and fear can't coexist
in the same realm without discordantly inconsistent harmonies.
She reminded me again to look for all the good of this experience
because that was in the here and now where God lives and love reigns
supreme. "Fear cannot rule in the present moment," Carol Margaret
emotes in her didactic fashion. And I knew from past experiences
(which at the time of aha were present moment awareness's gifts)
that everything always gets better so I could let go of the whole fear
thing and choose to embrace this new life without my longtime
companion. I wondered how Hilda was, where she had gone, and

Maggie suggested we pray for her eternally blissful and forever retirement in the wild with all other departed animals of our experience. Thank you, Maggie.

This section of my story is devoted to many of the goods that came from Hilda and brought good, God, and love as central to my vision for living, learning, loving, and serving with the gift of my precious life. Maggie suggests I title this first chapter of "The Goods" with the event that inspired the creation of this book ...

CHAPTER 12

Oh Good! She's Gone!

Imagine hosting a relative who isn't the easiest house guest and comes to visit for long enough that it becomes almost impossible to be gracious. However, best efforts prevail and the arduous times are endured with initially reluctant, albeit conscious acceptance. Or consider a rough bout of chicken pox in a very large family, where one child gets sick just as another recovers ... Each example requiring long, laborious processes of patience, hospitality, caregiving, service, and the gifts of smiles and kindness, which hosts and caregivers don't always feel like giving. Recall the feelings of fatigue, relief, and desire for renewal when the relative is gone or the last child is finally healthy and off to school? Those are the feelings I felt in the weeks after learning of Hilda's departure: kind of numb, grateful, and full of wanting to put this particular adventure behind me. How to do so was the all-consuming question. I had lived with this elephant for so long that I couldn't remember who I was before she arrived to displace me as the author of the book, captain of the ship, conductor of the symphony, keeper of the family.

The aftermath of her abandonment, although longed for, was almost a call for a "reinvention intervention" with myself. Not to mention, in the years she graced my life, I had aged into someone I no longer recognized. I was an empty nester now—no kids at home—and the only star demanding my attention and care on the Roth child or animal scene was beloved Brown Dog. Number One Husband was back to life as usual (whatever that meant with extreme metamorphoses in actual lifestyle and work modes), and I was living in the small town far away from our former large city, friends, and family. I had only experienced physical imbalance, grief, and financial stress in this small town, and although I loved the beauty, peace, and serenity of our cottage on the lake, I had no sense of how to reengage with life in terms of what possibilities were important to me: opportunities for service, following my bliss, creating connections, interacting with likeminded, open-hearted community, and fully, freely expressing my talents and gifts for the highest good of my life, at one with everyone around me. I was at square one, without an elephant, and filled with a sense of wonder and awe that I was in this position at all.

Maggie suggested we get really committed to daily practice of happy dances, journaling, walks, and prayer. Discernment of how to be elephant-free and thrive would come to us with patient and perseverant practice, she believed. I always listen to Maggie—except when I don't—so I developed consistent spiritual practice. I let go of trying to figure everything about life without Hilda and surrendered to spirit for guidance and direction.

As time unfolded, it became increasingly clear that an elephant-free Carol Margaret Hohlfelder Roth (a.k.a., *all donor*) was destined to live in our former large city. Although our tenants, who paid rent and had no intention of buying or maintaining our home in which they lived, still had months left on their lease, we owned a unique rental property in one of my favorite neighborhoods in our former large city. This unique (and only slightly larger than the cottage on the lake in our small town) home boasted a front porch with a swing and charming arches, hardwood floors, and lots of windows. When it was available, I told Number One Husband that I desired to move there. We shared some discordant and divisive conversation about my decision, and although he wrestled with the living arrangement dilemma (his business presence was required in the small town), he finally supported my decision to take Brown Dog to our former large city to make our home there. Number One Husband planned to commute when he could and possibly remove himself from his daily, in-person business responsibilities.

The furniture and possessions we had stored when we moved into the cottage on the lake in the small town were unearthed, and we moved them to the unique property in our former large city with a rental truck and several helpers. I was especially delighted to reunite with my piano, which I had not played during the time we lived at the cottage. My dreams and visions for my life expanded into reality.

I got involved with people and groups I loved. I started playing the piano again. I grew strong enough to walk Brown Dog. I got to see Elder Son and Great Girlfriend more often. I felt so happy, free, and creative. I could truly imagine anything. Every dream became possible!

In summer that year, my third year after transplant, during a regular visit to the favorite transplant docs, I graduated to medication free and yearly anniversary visits for smiles, hugs, and hellos. This hallmark occasion prompted an especially joyful happy dance and a celebration with Number One Husband.

We received a call from our tenants who paid rent, had no intention of buying or maintaining our home, and who, we had painfully discovered, terrorized our neighbors with their wildly unsupervised children and unruly animals' frequent trespasses. In fact, the neighbors on each side of our home had erected tall fences to block out this terrorizing tenant crew. We were mortified by the entire situation. ("But they pay rent," Carol Margaret reminds us.) These "exemplary" tenants told us they'd decided to move and would vacate the home in two months.

Number One Husband and I decided this new life we were creating did not need or want another residence, let alone a home and yard requiring a constant abundance of maintenance. We told the paying rent and non-maintaining tenants we'd like to see the home so we could list it for sale as soon as prudent or possible.

What an absolute shock our viewing was! Everything was broken, battered, dirty … Trees, bushes, plants, yard destroyed. Holes in ceilings, closet doors missing, cabinets—Maggie interrupts me. "Let's not get worked up. Look forward to how it all works out for good." The gist of the whole scenario: the condition was bad enough that we couldn't sell it as it was and get any money from it. It required money to restore it to a potentially saleable commodity, and it also needed a lot of time, work, and attention. We had the time, could do the work, and we could give the home our attention. The money part was the complication of this situation. It was challenging to see anything good about this fiasco. What to do?

Number One Husband and I had said good-bye to this house four years before. After much discussion, debate, tears, and frustration, we decided to say hello and call it home again. Our sickening good-bye to our tenants was such a horrible growth in awareness that it can't be shared without reliving its awfulness. Suffice it to say, we're so glad we got through the tenant removal and began the intensive repair, painting, cleaning, replacing, and planting and all the work required to heal our home. "And look how the light shines through the windows!" Carol Margaret and Maggie admire the sunshine streaming through the glass as I step back from my window-washing perch on the step ladder. It was and is a work in progress, but I could do what I could do elephant-free! Helping our home to heal was a bit like a stem cell transplant in a very general and concrete, nonhuman form. Very grateful I was for my past adventure with Hilda. This home reinvention was a walk in the park compared to my failed attempts to walk on the water with Hilda. "You're learning ..." Maggie says as a sunbeam dances on the wall.

In spite of all the work, money, and maintenance, it felt good to be back where we had a history and could enjoy our todays and tomorrows. We still had the same wonderful neighbors who had been terrorized by the tenants, and I promised myself I would make amends in any way possible. To my relief, they were so happy for our return that it became necessary to transfer our happy dancing stage to the cul-de-sac so all of our neighbors could join us.

It felt good to be in our home without Hilda. It was fun to be strong enough to work in the yard again, to live in a house where we could invite as many people as we wanted to invite for dinner, meetings, or whatever and have room for all of them. We loved hosting friends for meals and fellowship. Sunsets and sunrises were beautiful from our sunroom, windows, or yard. Nature and wildlife were center stage. My heart was full of love and gratitude for a real home again and thanksgiving for the memories we had created and were creating here. Brown Dog gleefully remembered the big yard, circling it with joyful exuberance, chasing squirrels with immense delight. "Welcome home, Brown Dog," the squirrels seemed to taunt as they teased and scurried from tree to fence to grass, giving Brown Dog quite the workout. Brown Dog's gladness inspired us as we followed our aging and exceedingly charming Labrador retriever around the yard in a happy jog, no elephant behind us.

CHAPTER 13

Good Girl

Donor

In the aftermath of Hilda, when we finally determined her hopefully permanent retreat, the question of wondering and waiting to discover Donor's identity was suddenly over and much more than a wonder and wait. We could learn his/her name and other information if we wanted to put a name, a face, and a voice on the person who significantly contributed to my healthy new self. Donor was a unique, original—the only person on the registry who even kind of matched me. "An angel!" Maggie reverently calls the donor. "Thank you, Angel." Maggie and I raise our arms high. Carol Margaret looks at us as if we've lost our minds and reminds us to thank God first. "Thank you, God." The three of us solemnly bow our heads and sincerely express our gratitude to God, Donor, our favorite transplant docs, family, friends, and Hilda. It's all good!

Donor had written to me that he/she would meet me, if I wanted to meet him/her. My imagination had created all kinds of scenarios about meeting him/her, what he/she would be like, where he/she lived, and if he were a he or she were a she. It was confusing at best, and because Donor is a gender neutral term of pure possibility, perhaps my imagination and Donor's anonymity might be preferable to full disclosure, conversation, and meeting. How could I begin to thank Donor for this gift of healing he/she had given me? Wasn't praying for him/her enough? All of the "whelmings" zoomed on the horizon, and I just wanted to go hide out under my blanket.

I waited to contact Donor until Hilda was totally gone. I worried Donor would feel responsible for my less than beautifully healthy physical body, and a good girl, according to Carol Margaret, did not intentionally worry people. My over-responsible self had come out to wrestle with me via Carol Margaret, and I found myself wondering why I kept getting to confront all these good girl rules. Maggie reminded me that I was good, no matter what, and that we could get really still and discover the best way to decide what to do and how to do it. So we did.

The next time I visited our favorite transplant center, I asked to find out the name and phone number of Donor. One of my favorite transplant nurses said he would call me with the name and number when he received it. I was truly excited when I learned that Donor was a she, lived in the same state, had the same first name as Super Sister, and was about the same age as I was, and had been married a year longer than I and Number One Husband.. I was nervous when I called her on the phone, and we began a forever soul sister friendship. We enjoyed phone conversations and e-mails before we decided to meet in the fall after Number One Husband and I had moved back to our real home, three years post-transplant. We picked a restaurant located about halfway between the cities where we lived and agreed to meet for lunch on a crisp, sunny morning.

I got to the restaurant early ("Good girls are never late." Carol Margaret quotes only mother and porch-swinging grandmother). I searched for the best placed booth for soulful connection and waited and wondered until she arrived with a smile. We hugged, cried, laughed, and spent hours in that now-holy place sharing our hearts and our stories. Donor was a grandmother—which, to my great delight, had become my happy title a few weeks earlier. We were about the same height, and our waitress thought we were sisters. When we finally and somewhat reluctantly left the restaurant to drive to our respective homes, we discovered we drove identical automobiles. A very special day we shared, one I will never forget! I love you, Donor, my good and forever sister friend!

Delight

I can't begin to contain the incredible joy, mind-expanding power, and bubble-blowing freedom I felt post-transplant and all the good I witnessed, expressed, and realized in every facet of my living. The world and everything in it sparkle and shine, no matter what! Maggie inspired me to find delight (except when I don't) with cleaning the grossest, grimiest, dirtiest parts of everything. I'm grateful to pay bills, run even laborious errands, do massive loads of laundry, scrub floors and toilets, walk in the cold, wet, and wind, organize all that's disorganized, wait in line for hours ... My list of "love tos" is infinite because I'm alive, blessed, whole, and well, and I can do most or all of these things, a Hurrah—at least some of the time. When Carol Margaret is her analytical, judgmental worst, I falter in this absolute bliss. Maggie suggests we attempt to practice integrating and accepting all parts of me, to look for the good in the Carol Margaret piece and help her to let go of the fear that keeps her from seeing good, love, and God in everything and everyone all of the time.

The only obstacles in the way of good, love, and God are the pretend, make- believe falsities, Carol Margaret's pontifications, -which I truly consider to be my limiting fears of what people will think about me- and my inaccurate, fallacious, highly subjective fears of bad and wrong things happening in my world. When I protect myself or utilize offensive or defensive attacks, when I don't comprehend something/someone different from me, when I remain with the confines of my familiar, narrow, coffin-like box, I refuse new experience and become unequipped to fully experience a cancer-free life. "No way to embrace delight with that fearful behavior!" We nod our heads in agreement.

After living with uncertainty, in my waiting, wondering, watching, surrendering control mode of Hilda co-existence; with giving up my need to understand or interpret, and detaching from my situation to live into the questions; whenever I start to judge, analyze, compare, or run away; I'm finally learning that delightful living is as simple as my choice, and I don't need or want those festive accoutrements and complexities that go with my mental machinations. I can consciously choose to discover any way I can to live with the delight of knowing that all things are possible, including love, peace, and good intention by all of creation. We get to let go of the bad, the wrong, and seek the good, love, and God in everything, ("No matter what!" Maggie agrees).

I often walk and daydream about what the world could be like if we were in union with this miraculous way of living. Sometimes Maggie and I start our skip, gallop, jump routine and launch our uncontrollable giggling onslaught at the ongoing presence of miracles. I wouldn't wish health issues or other debilitating challenges on anyone, but I'm grateful my life experiences have brought this amazing method of delighting in the infinite goodness of our world and voraciously searching for it in every conscious experience.

My earthly father liked to recite the poem about the wise old owl. I have particularly delighted in a young great horned owl that was born and raised near our backyard. As the owlet matured, the owl grew quieter, observed more, and grew more resourceful with owl like pursuits before leaving home, relocating to stomping grounds far away from the mother that birthed, fed, taught, and nurtured new life.

> The wise owl sat on the oak.
> The more the owl saw, the less the owl spoke.
> The less the owl spoke, the more the owl heard.
> Why can't we be like that wise owl bird?

Delight, of light, is good—even for owls learning to primarily hunt in the darkness, dusks, and dawns of life—the unclear, dim, unseen places. Life has darkness, and most of creation doesn't have owl vision to compensate. The light within is always shining and illumines dark moments when I look for the good as I sit, watch, listen, and pray. "How delightful!" Maggie exclaims.

Desire

Three questions I often ask myself as I prepare to meditate are, "Who am I? What do I want? What is my dharma/purpose?" These are questions I express inside myself before I empty thought and focus on a mantra or my breath. What I find fascinating is how, after my meditation time, my day unfolds into the living of those three questions, all of which create conscious choices in the unfolding of those questions into what I desire to vision for my life and my world. I get to vision responsibly in a playground of continual questioning, and as I wait, watch, listen, and wonder, life unfolds as I choose and act from the interplay of my questions with circumstance, response, intention, and vision. Maggie calls the synchronicities of these days "thanksgiving miracles of spirit." I choose an appropriate attitude and behavior in accordance with what I want, who I choose to be, and how I perceive my responsibility in whatever situation I find myself, and I give thanks.

When I am congruent, I am in union with the highest good, which means I'm integrating what I choose to be, to do, and to have with what matters to me, forming "my truth." When I am responsibly in alignment with my purpose, I am at one with the highest good, for all creation. This part of my chosen formula really resonates with Carol Margaret's need to have an explanation for everything. When I operate in integrity and congruence, in accord with what I hold dear and true, the world shines brighter. My healing embrace of what is true, honorable, just, pure, lovely, and gracious brings more of what I desire to enhance the blessing of goodness, God, and love on this planet. "And that's good!" Carol Margaret struggles with this judgment thing. Maggie prefers to hear Carol Margaret's statement as a blessing of our shared desire to transform and bloom into the goodness that already is. "Good point, Maggie!" So much good everywhere … What's a good girl to do?

Now that I have this gift of delight in everything and the miracles created for my life with embrace of the questions, I could move past the good girl ideology of my younger years and grow that into completely sharing what I've learned, how I've loved, and the amazing gifts of life with Hilda and now, without her. Now is the time to share the good gifts of our adventure with everyone around me.

"All good gifts …" Maggie starts into another song. Thank you, Godspell.

CHAPTER 14

Good Gifts

Blankets

My adventure with Hilda, like much of my life, included letting go. I don't just mean letting go … I mean *letting go*, and letting go and letting go again. In my physical spiritual life, even as a little girl, it was painful to let go of that to which I was attached. It began with something like a favorite blanket my only mother threw away one day. My only mother liked to clean up and throw things away in her free time, perhaps a book I had stacked somewhere it didn't belong. I loved to read, especially in my closet, in my parents' closet, or under the piano. My only mother was very good at keeping order and believed cleanliness was next to godliness. One thing I was careful never to leave lying around was my third-grade Bible. I carefully tucked it away each day and slept with it every night. When times were tough, I talked to Jesus, and this red, Revised Standard Version holy book went almost everywhere with me, kind of like Jesus was holding my hand, and because I was a rather, weird precocious little girl ("If you're not a little weird, you're boring," says Maggie.), Jesus got to hold my hand a lot. I always loved blankets, and when I went away to college, my porch-swinging grandmother knit me an afghan in my favorite shades of blue.

My beloved grandmother also gave me my favorite great aunt's crocheted blanket, where each square was unique and different than any other. My favorite great aunt died when I was in middle school, and I held on to this blanket as a remembrance of her and the gifts of love, faith, and fun she brought to my life. The idea that my beloved porch-swinging grandmother had put her gifts to good use making those beautiful blankets inspired my attachment to them. I wished that I, too, could be crafty or talented enough to knit, crochet, or cook like my beloved grandmother. She patiently tried to teach me all of those skills and the game of bridge to no avail. What she did teach me is the sacredness of the simple and the ordinary, of giving the gift of self, welcoming everyone, hospitality, service, caring, and God at the center of every experience. She made Elder Son's and Younger Son's baby blankets. She made a blanket for Number One Husband. And she made blankets for the babies I dreamed about, too.

My porch-swinging grandmother moved to a nursing home the year Hilda officially came to live with me. My only mother suggested we not share my diagnosis because only mother's father, my porch-swinging grandmother's husband, had died from an elephant similar to Hilda. When at 102 years of age, my porch-swinging grandmother was dying in a hospital ("Something had to get her, remember?" says Carol Margaret when she thinks I might be teary), I covered my beloved grandmother with a warm blanket, pulled out my tattered red book, and began to read to her Psalm 23. She gazed at me serenely and joyfully joined me word for word in her recitation of a favorite scripture. I am grateful for her life, and I am attached to that memory as a great gift.

Shortly before my transplant, the red Bible disintegrated. I could no longer turn the fragile, loved, and tear-stained pages. A fabulous friend offered to loan me her red Revised Standard Version Bible because she knew how attached I was to mine. I was touched by her thoughtfulness. My One Husband offered to spend hundreds of dollars to get my worn-out book rebound. Everyone was worried about how I'd get through this adventure without my symbolic manifestation of holding Jesus's hand.

It dawned on me that red book, while loved, was only one expression of comfort, grace, love, and my friend, Jesus. My grandmother was another. They may not be physically with me, but I am connected to them eternally. I could buy another Bible, underline all my favorite passages, and inscribe all our family's auspicious dates and dashes. The actual thing of that particular red book wasn't necessary to hold onto. Its memory, smell, texture, words—all were with me without the physical thing, just like my porch-swinging grandmother.

As I thought more about material things to which I attached, I also pondered this upcoming transplant and all the things in my life. I did not need all of these things. I could survive without my favorite blanket and my favorite book. What could life be like if I gave away things before I became too attached to them? This mode of thinking created an opportunity to play a fun game with myself and give away some of the stuff I loved to people I love. ("Just don't do the Pollyanna thing, just don't!" Carol Margaret barks.) I realize that what I have loved about these knickknacks, jewelry, books, odds and ends, artwork ... were the sentiments associated with the givers and the memories of receiving them. I loved picking things I loved during that time before transplant to gift to people I loved. I shared why I gave them my significant something, and I found as much or perhaps more joyous delight in regifting these crystal paperweights, china collectibles, furniture, and jewelry to persons I loved. And I felt freedom, grace, and the room to grow in the release of all my stuff. Thank you, simplicity, acceptance, and inspiration!

Blankets, especially blue ones, were a big part of Hilda. One of the Roth Labrador retrievers chewed a hole in my porch-swinging grandmother's blue blanket, so it became hol (e) y to me in more than one way, but not the world's greatest option for staying warm. I was especially careful with my favorite great aunt's crocheted blanket because it was one of a kind. I indulged my love for blue blankets before beginning treatment again after my four-year vacation from Hilda by purchasing a large, soft, fleece-like and exceptionally warm and comforting blanket. I took it to treatment every time for years, from my first trainer's chemo corral, to the integrated cancer center and back again.

When I was enjoying one of my last regular chemotherapies, the winter before the decision to board the elephant truck, I was waiting for Number One Husband to pick me up from the corral, and I forgot to keep track of my blanket. I was feeling the after-effect of treatment when I left the corral, and it didn't occur to me it was missing until days later. I called and searched everywhere, to no avail.

Many months later when we began our three months of shots in the belly, I arrived to the chemo corral, to discover that a baldly beautiful sleeping patient in the corner of the room was artfully covered with my missing blue blanket. I remarked to one of my frequent nurse caregivers that I had been looking for the blanket for months and thought I'd lost it. She remarked dismissively that she'd taken it home to wash it, and they needed blankets. When I left, I felt disturbed that she didn't offer to give me my blanket back. If she would have offered, I would have said, "No, please keep it." However, she didn't ask, and I felt really icky about that omission. "Another opportunity to assess the need to assess," Carol Margaret grumbles.

As I mentioned previously, our kind neighbor, from next door to our cottage on the lake, made me a beautiful blanket, colorful on one side and deep blue, like the lake, on the other. During the first weeks of my transplant conditioning and treatment, that blanket was as much a part of me as my arms and legs. It was my constant companion, much like my red book and childhood blanket. Favorite transplant nurses joked that my positive attitude came from my magic blanket. It sparked smiles and good conversation, for which I was grateful.

One of our favorite transplant nurses was going through a rough time in her life and decided to leave her position at our favorite transplant center. She became rather teary as she shared her situation. We had loved her sparkle, caring, curiosity, and wit. We would miss her. Spontaneously, I thrust my magic blue blanket at her and told her to take it for as long as she needed it. She assured me she would keep it only awhile and then bring it back to me. I suggested she could do that, keep it, or she could gift it to someone else when her need for it was gone.

I was committed to non-attachment; but in the meantime, I was really cold, and I kind of wondered if I'd thought this nonattachment thing through for the highest good. Kind neighbor's sister realized I was cold while waiting and wondering if the blue blanket would come back, so she made me another blanket, a pink one with butterflies. Although it wasn't blue, it was warm, and I felt graced and grateful.

As my transplant journey approached winter, I wondered aloud to Number One Husband how complicated making fleece blankets would be. Number One Husband, knowing my less-than-stellar craftiness, exhaled a large guffaw. When I looked at him seriously and asked again, he suggested we ask kind neighbor's sister to show us how it was done. Elder Son's birthday was impending. We would make his blanket as our first experimental project. Maggie suggested she would contribute extra prayers so that the blanket could be done in excellence for the birthday guy. We received our lessons, and it was especially challenging to me because of the weakness and wrenching arthritis in my fingers, hands, wrists, arms ("Your whole body!" Carol Margaret corrects me.) from the graft versus host disease still wrenching my fragile frame.

We would trim the fleece, make tag-like cuts around the blanket, and tie the cut tags with our prayers for Elder Son on the blanket we would make. I struggled with the scissors and couldn't figure out the technique to make the knots in the blanket.

Number One Husband assisted me in tying a knot in Elder Son's birthday blanket so I could say I'd contributed. I was frustrated I couldn't do more, but Maggie encouraged me to pray and set a vision for all the amazing prayer blankets I could make for loved ones in the future. I yearned for that freedom of ability, act of service vision, so I gave thanks and kept praying, dreaming, and believing it always gets better. "Good job!" Carol Margaret affirmed in a businesslike fashion with a slight smile of acknowledgment for my positive, forward-moving thinking.

Number One Husband, knowing how drawn I was to big blue blankets, weaved his prayers for me into an especially beautiful blue blanket of his creation. I felt so loved and embraced by possibility. His gifted blanket was my childhood equivalent of holding hands with Jesus ("With your current theology, holding hands with First Grandson, Pastor Carolyn, Ganesh, or your swami of the day would be comparable, *n'est-ce-pas?*") Carol Margaret and Maggie find ways for union with all the important ideas in life. Thank you, ladies. I treasured that blanket so much I gave it to Donor when we met almost three years later. Thank you, Number One Husband!

Elder Son and I were big fans of our blankets, so I persuaded Number One Husband to help me make more for all of our family. I would pick out the material and say the prayers while he cut and tied, always saving a small section for my contribution. As I became stronger, I learned to cut and tie on my own. My first solo blanket was a surprise for Number One Husband's birthday the year I learned Hilda was gone.

I found so much joy making these blankets ("Small things with great love," Maggie remarks thoughtfully.) that I became a regular at imagining what material I would order or buy and what prayers I would pray for each person as I made his/her blanket. It became a holy mission, pouring prayers, loving thoughts, blessings, and good wishes into these creations Carol Margaret considered "almost crafty." Everyone in our family received a blanket the next few years especially created for them. I felt so connected to my porch-swinging grandmother because I used my hands and heart to send love and prayers to those I loved.

It was an incredible joy, three years post-transplant, to tie little blankets for First Grandson. His birth that year, his new life, my elephant-free, living presence in it, my beyond overwhelming love and blessing for this "Sweetie Pie Honey Bunny" is one of the greatest gifts of post-Hilda living. I get to be Grammy! Thank you, God! Needless to say, First Grandson has more blankets than any other family member, using them for forts, outside play, and cuddle and sleep time, and he even brings them with him when he comes to our home for slumber parties.

Dear friends and their families had birthdays, illnesses, or appreciation for warmth and loving wishes, so I expanded my ministry to include blankets for them at appropriate moments in their lives. I prayed for them when I picked out material and when I cut tags and tied knots in the tags of the blanket. My friends appreciate them, and I appreciate the connection that the tied prayers in blanket form represent for us. "Blest be the tie that binds ..." Maggie launches into an old hymn she particularly loved singing in one of her favorite plays, "Our Town."

As our first full year of not visiting our favorite transplant docs approached our four-year transplant anniversary date, I was experiencing optimal wellness, great energy, and exuberant happiness. I made the decision not to schedule a wellness check up to confirm what I already knew to be true for me: I am well, and Hilda is gone! "Amen!" Maggie and Carol Margaret repeat our affirmation of blessing in unison. It looked like my visit to the favorite transplant center would be for smiles, hugs, and hellos. Maggie came up with a great idea when Carol Margaret suggested that good girls do not arrive empty-handed and must come bearing gifts. Maggie encouraged me to make blankets for prospective transplant patients, tying knots of prayers for blessing and wellness, support, encouragement, and hope into their blankets. Because we had been under the care of the transplant center for three years, we chose to make three blankets. Actually, we made two, and I laundered the one blue blanket I had made the year before because it contained the majority of prayers I had prayed that year. After giving away that first blue blanket four years earlier, I learned self-care necessitated making a blanket for myself as well, so the third blanket I made for myself, to be given to a future transplant recipient the next year. My personal blankets were always blue, but recognizing others may appreciate other colors, I included a variety of colors in the blankets I made. Maggie suggested we make a back-up blanket as well so we could always have a back-up to give as spirit moved us. It was delightful, meaningful, and fun for me to make those blankets, write anonymous notes to go with them, and write a letter to all the favorite transplant docs, favorite transplant nurses, and employees to thank them for everything. Because all of them were busy with patients and caregiving, I left my good gifts at the office and saved the hugs and hellos for the next time. I did get to smile, though, and that was a very good feeling.

From that point on, I started praying for struggling people I didn't know when I heard about them. I journaled my prayers every morning and made blankets for people I didn't know when I would hear about them. Very often, I would learn that the blanket that the person I didn't know, but had heard about, received from my prayers were his/her favorite colors or design. "Prayer is powerful." All three of us agree.

For year five of my transplant anniversary, I made an appointment to see Dr. Gloom and Doom because routine blood tests at my new internist had shown some abnormalities, and I felt unusually tired.

Armed with three blankets for year five, I journeyed to the newer, bigger hospital also named after one of my favorite Christian saints on the south side of my large city, where my favorite transplant docs had moved their offices two years before this visit. I was greeted with smiles, hugs, and hellos. Dr. Gloom and Doom suggested that because Hilda included many transfusions, I had a surplus of iron in my body. The remedy was called therapeutic phlebotomy. (Number One Husband and Carol Margaret outrageously chortle, "What he means is a lobotomy, Carol!" They love to give me a hard time.) This procedure was a blood-letting: a unit of blood would be removed from me monthly for as long as it took to improve the blood numbers, and then, the blood was thrown away in the health-approved-for-blood garbage can. The "iron"y of this development was twofold: First, before the transplant, the donor had a temporary iron deficiency, which was the obstacle she overcame before donating to me. Second, my painfully unrealized yearning to donate blood to others was in my face again. "This situation is truly ironic," Carol Margaret snorted as Maggie stroked my arm.

This monthly procedure could take place at any infusion center. I briefly thought of visiting ultimate infectious disease doc's office closer to my home, but when I learned he'd retired earlier that year, I embraced my return to the favorite transplant center in the bigger, newer, named after the favorite Christian saint hospital with monthly appointments for therapeutic phlebotomy.

Maggie encouraged me to consider this unfolding a good gift because it could be an opportunity to reconnect with some very awesome people ("Make more blankets." Carol Margaret already has us in doing mode.) and to celebrate the fact that this imbalance isn't Hilda. To confirm the absolute knowing that Hilda had no role in this latest development, Dr. Gloom and Doom advised that we do one very final "who's who" test. He shared that if this test were negative, we would probably never need to do another one. I whispered a good-bye to avoiding my full deductible payment, with a thank you to medical insurance, and agreed to the test. Maggie suggested we remember our resident great horned owl and behave according to the lessons we learned from observing owl behavior and ways of being. I decided to be silly. "*Who-who.*" Carol Margaret collapses in disgust as Maggie joins me with owl sounds. We mutually agree to watch, wait, and wonder as we post on our perch over the health horizon.

I especially loved and appreciated several awesomely wonderful transplant nurses whose favorite colors I discovered before making them blankets with my gratitude and blessing tied into the tags. It was much nicer to travel for treatment bearing good gifts and well wishes, I thought. It became especially joyful when the "who's who" test came back *all donor*! Our happy dance was perfected at this point. "Grateful and Graced" Maggie twirls on her toes as she proclaims our state of wonder.

To think those little things like blankets and other good gifts can be opportunities for service inspires me. From my childhood blanket to my porch-swinging grandmother's afghans; to a purchased blue blanket, a symbol of comfort and warmth for healing; to the gift of a cut, tied, and knotted fleece blanket made by a kind neighbor, and of course, never forgetting my beloved red book—I know I experienced these gifts as coverings of grace, prayer, warmth, protection, blessing, and love. To be able to share those gifts with others increases that blessing for me. I get to give from the good gifts I've received. Thank you "once upon a time!" "All good gifts around us are sent from heaven above ..." one of Maggie's and Super Sister's favorite songs erupts in full voice from a grateful Maggie. (Carol Margaret prefers this musical rendition to our hooting.) Thank you, good gifts!

Blessings

A rather frequent to do, I've been told, is to count my blessings. I've also been told I am blessed to be a blessing. "What I put out from inside me determines my reality ..." Maggie is blessed with the good gift of awful rhyming. Carol Margaret comments on the blessing of my positive spin on judgmental evaluation. I assure her I appreciate the blessing of her being, probably, right about almost everything.

One way I've learned to bless in my quest to be a blessing is found in the word, *bless*: "B (e) *less*." "Not as in diminished, tiny, or not as good ..." Carol Margaret is quick to clarify. "Rather, to 'b less' means to be humble, put something reverently before one's own self-interest, and lift it up to God with thanksgiving and prayer." Carol Margaret loves to be definitive. When I explore the experience of sharing my "blessedness" into the act of "b lessing," I recognize that the times I bless become true blessing when I'm humble, vulnerable, outward and/or upward focused, surrendered, authentic, and present in the moment of whatever is, no matter if I'm broken, lost, hurting, fragile, fatigued, ecstatic, overflowing, joyful, grateful, or happy dancing. When I am less Carol Margaret Hohlfelder Roth and more of a channel for good/love/God, a little bit of me can go a long way in the blessing department. Maggie takes this opportunity to burst into one of her favorite Melissa Etheridge songs, "And the world goes round and round and round ... a little bit of you in a little bit of me ..."

To reference my years with Hilda, there were many opportunities to share my "b lessedness," although much of the time I was a reluctant, unaware, and resistant b lesser. It is only upon reflection and feedback from others' experiences of me on differing occasions that I learned how my vulnerability actually blessed people who knew me. While Carol Margaret deplores the whole vulnerable thing, Maggie reminds me to think of Jesus, who showed us the b lessing of true strength through surrender and vulnerability. Easier said than done, and I masked so much of my vulnerable parts until I couldn't anymore. "That's when the real b lessing of Hilda happened," Maggie asserts with confidence.

I enjoyed reading a favorite poem recently that compares our lives to Homer's "Odyssey." Odysseus' adventures parallel our journey of growth to authenticity, the expression of our complete self, and an actualization of our calling to bring our blessedness to be a blessing.

"Ithaka"

As you set out in search of Ithaka, pray that your journey be long, full of adventures, full of awakenings ...

Carol Margaret likes this poem because it was a favorite of Jackie O's. ("A true lady." Carol Margaret has a bit of an obsession with admirable celebrities she considers of relevance.) Maggie likes this poem because she loves the idea of life as a journey to authenticity. Thank you, C. P. Cavafy! "Where good, love, and God live is where we travel!" Carol Margaret exclaims. "And we are always supported and guided safely home by good, love, and God!" Maggie adds broadly. What a blessing their proclamations are to my discovery travels!

The discovery I'm uncovering in my relationship with Maggie is that all my blessings contribute to the benison of the planet. Carol Margaret clasps her hands in delight that I'm using a word Younger Son has blessed us with in our quest for an expanding vocabulary. Maggie, slightly bewildered, suddenly jumps up with a room-drenching smile of joy and exclaims, "The Beatitudes!" When Carol Margaret and I look at each other with shoulder shrugs, Maggie explains, "Sermon on the Mount ... the supreme blessings ... the 'benisons' of scripture ... The ways we are blessed to create our blessings!" We start to get it, and before erupting into our happy dancing mode, we pause to remember how richly grateful we are for these benisons. Thank you, God.

In considering Maggie's reference to the Beatitudes, I thought about this particular scripture and what it means to me. As I ponder these eight ways to transform my perception of experience, I realize the Beatitudes are also the *be attitudes*. If I want to be pure in heart, I get to release worry and choose to see good, love, and God. If I want peace and forgiveness, I get to be peaceful and forgiving. When I feel sad, frustrated or discouraged, I get to pray, search for good, love, and God, and I always, eventually, feel good, love, and God.

When I endeavor to b less my beingness into what I seek to create in my experience, I evolve into that which I aspire to be. By choosing an intentional way of being to transform my experience, b lessing what I am, and trusting in the alchemy that is possibility, abundant blessing upon blessing graces my world. When I feel afraid, I get to move through my fears to good, love, and God.

If someone treats me with less than the respect and kindness I deserve as a beloved creation of the Source who made me, I get to b less them and know that I am good and loved and the next moment isn't the previous one. I get to *be* what I choose for my attitude to be, and when I consciously adopt that process, my life transforms. Carol Margaret quickly peruses the fifth chapter of Matthew in our newer black Bible ("Verses 1 through 11," she further defines) as she begins to design assorted ways we can incorporate this supremely blessed doctrine into our experience of Hilda. Maggie looks at her with compassion and suggests we simply "be" the attitude we want to own for ourselves and leave the rest to the Sower of Dreams. I so admire the many names Maggie gives good, love, and God. Thank you for creative variety, Maggie. The gifts of life with Hilda were learning to be positive, to be grateful, to be hopeful, and to be intentional … whatever we wanted to experience, we chose to be with our attitude.

So, we determined, we get to "be less," to "be attitude," and then Carol Margaret, in her usual assertive, image-conscious, and superficially material fashion, suggests, "Beautiful!" Maggie tweaks her idea and with a unique flair finishes, "Be you to full!" Carol Margaret wants to say, "Full of it, for sure," but the look I give her silences her voicing of less than true, honest, inspiring, nice, or kind remarks, as she decides to model our owl and perch on her figurative oak for an intellectual time-out to think.

Be you to full ... was the authenticity journey of my life even before Hilda, an arduous, laborious, painful, yet rewarding road to travel. When Elder Son was a rebellious teen, he and I were face-to-face in the kitchen, engaged in a heated discussion about his perceived entitlements (curfew, money, girls, outings with friends, etc.) when the phone rang. I answered it to hear the voice of someone whose opinion mattered to me. I became effusive, flattering, laughing; solely focused on the person at the other end of the phone; totally ignoring the uncomfortable energy permeating the space I still shared with Elder Son. When I finally hung up the phone, Elder Son glared at me and accused me of being fake, saying he didn't like who I was.

Deeply disturbed by his feedback, I consciously decided I would be my true self in every situation. If I were present with someone in intense conversation, I would not abandon our conversation to answer the phone. Even if the person I choose to be doesn't please or agree with the person with whom I am in relationship, I commit to developing acceptance of my being as congruent, authentic, and present in every facet of my life. I would like to say I was totally successful with this endeavor from the beginning, but I wasn't. It is an ongoing process, like forgiveness, that takes patience, perseverance, and all manner of other assorted attributes that often abandon me in moments of fatigue, hunger, stress, anger, boredom, or loneliness.

Hilda was a huge gift of growth for me in the *be you to full* aspiration because, with Hilda, especially the last few years, being my authentic self, inside and out, was all I could be. And as far as the word *beautiful* applied to my physical appearance, I never felt more the antithesis of beautiful than in those pervasive moments when Hilda smothered my ability to celebrate any avenue that led me to viewing a friendly mirror. Before Hilda, I was more focused on what I looked like—hair, clothes, figure, and makeup. Luckily, except for sporadic moments in time, the mirror and I were friends. The awareness I discover, upon reflection, is that those moments the mirror and I were *not* friends were the moments that remained front row center pre-Hilda. ("Nonreflective glass," Maggie mutters.) Carol Margaret suggests that all people struggle to accept themselves and seek opportunities for self-flagellation. "Just don't!" she lectures me.

Somehow, and it must have been the be less, be attitude gifts, I stopped measuring myself as much by the mirror or by what other people thought of me. "What other people think of me is none of my business!" Thank you, Byron Katie. Hilda inspired me to choose to accept myself, however I showed up, as lovable, good, and full of possibilities. To my mirror, I am truly beautiful when I embrace the fullness I am. "Truly *be you … to full.*" Maggie winks. A day without makeup is freeing. The number on the scale is irrelevant. If my hair looks awful, at least I can smile, laugh, skip, jump, sing, and shout: "I'm alive, and I'm here, now, and me!" Whoopee!

To inculcate and live abundantly these significant gifts of learning and loving from Hilda, I get to *be gin* ("Not as in a drink with lime and tonic, surely?" Carol Margaret raises her eyebrow with her mocking tongue in cheek.) Especially I aspire to be Gin Su, not as in the infamous knife commercials of yesteryear but rather a master of circumstance, as in a Gin Su fisherman (the one who catches all the fish). "Like Number One Husband," Maggie offers affirmatively. Carol Margaret suggests Gin as a genie thing, but when Maggie starts humming the "I Dream of Jeanie" theme song, we shake our heads *no*! We quickly abandon that frame of reference.

To be Gin is something I aim to embrace in every adventure. Inherent in all situations are the ability and opportunity to experience beginning and then to begin again and again and again. With Hilda, I learned that life is filled with beginnings that morph into more beginnings again and again and again and again, ad infinitum. An ending is merely the creation of enough room for another beginning. The word *begin* encourages us to beg in or ask into being. "Another in and up, and 'Ask, and it shall be given …'" Maggie and I link arms as we skip down the yellow brick road. Carol Margaret crosses her eyes and lumbers distractedly behind us, googling incessant queries on her smartphone.

One other significant uncovered blessing came from a "late-night-couldn't-sleep-thoughts-are-racing" imaginary conversation with Maggie and Carol Margaret. Discussing our German heritage, Maggie made a highly accented comment as she revealed one of our more significant gifts of Hilda's departure. We get to "*be* well" was her remark, but it came out *be vel.* Carol Margaret proceeded to do her googling (which Maggie and I attempt diligently to consider a benison), came up with the word *bevel,* and decided we could make "be vel" part of our gratitude/blessing because it could soften the edges, ease the transitions, and keep us nonperpendicular so we could always be cutting edge, safe, and weather resistant in an aesthetically pleasing manner as we maneuvered our way uniquely through our adventures. Maggie and I thought Carol Margaret might be trying too hard, but appreciating her efforts; we gave her a hug and called it a night with, "Bless you and I love you." Our conversation gifted me a smile, a yawn, and a snore. Thank you, Silly Imaginings.

The Never Written, Never Read Chapter

With Hilda gone, I can reflect on the gifts she gave me, and I realize I was blessed to encounter and experience a degree of self-examination I may not have ever recognized or chosen to embrace without her presence in my life. Because Hilda was enormous and with me for many years, there were no unfilled rooms to bury feelings or hide from myself. Self- examination became a necessary prerequisite for my healing adventure. When I became elephant-free, I could finally recognize Hilda as a great gift for an accelerated self-examination workshop. Although Hilda was unique to me, I imagine all of us have hidden or forgotten pieces of ourselves lodged within us. Consciously or unconsciously, these parts of ourselves wait to be retrieved and released, empowering us to grow who we are.

Carol Margaret calls the unexpressed, buried parts of ourselves that we either don't, won't, or can't share with others, "conditional ingredients". These ingredients are the pieces we store and pour into a pot with the rest of a creative expression, (in this case a culinary simile) like a soup, that simmers all of who we are, flavoring what we want, and how we serve it to the world. These private or secret recipes flavoring our soups unique to each of us aren't required to be gifted, sold, or shared with everyone—maybe no one or only our nearest and dearest, and then only *if* we choose to randomly or selectively gift our outsides these insides.

Sometimes what is buried within us is filed and cataloged in an organized cabinet with labeled manila folders and a numbered table of contents. Perhaps a painful memory or an unresolved dilemma gets pushed down under mountains of other stacks of unfiled issues we don't want to address, view, or list in our numbered table of contents. The problem is this procrastinated paperwork emerges to the top of the pile repeatedly, each time forcing us to decide whether to ignore or deal with whatever surprise, pain, shame or forgotten issue appears. "Once again, another choice point," we say with a sigh.

Maggie suggests that "the clutter we stuff encourages our 'not enough.'" (Maggie's rhyming attempt creates physical cringes of distaste from Carol Margaret.) As we explore that idea in our quest to bless, we come to the conclusion that stuffing, ignoring, hiding, separating, and being conditional affect every aspect of our being—our authenticity, congruence, integrity, self-acceptance, acts of service, and bevel and be attitude.

We don't beg-in or be Gin when we never start our query or ask our questions. The unexplored, dark particles can be ignored; but the decision, aware or unaware, to bury them stunts growth, wellness, and the conscious adoption of a life with goodness, grace, and love.

When I cook my soup, sharing my secret ingredients, pulling them out of hiding, washing, cutting, and chopping, and then mindfully choosing how to stir them into the culinary wonder that is Carol Margaret Hohlfelder Roth; I become inspired to soar a little higher, love a little deeper, connect with everything a bit wider, and feel a whole bunch freer. As I share my nonconditionally composed soup and its contents with another; perhaps, another's soup recipe, without condition, will be shared with me. "And that's how we feed the world!" Maggie raises her spoon triumphantly.

However, before we administer our collective recipes for healing the world, I get to be brave enough to get through all the obstacles that preclude a magical life of all that empowers and blesses good, love, and—"Oneness! We are one," Maggie interrupts. "Another name for God, perhaps?" Carol Margaret muses as she googles "names for God" on her iPad.

To make my "soup" (Maggie considers our soup to be the culinary equivalent of our soul song, a.k.a., my absolute becoming the full embodiment of who I am created to be), delicious and nutritious, I get to sort through all those hidden secrets and consciously glean what to spice and what to splice (Maggie literally gleams at that expression.). Time to declutter and live! "Be the change. Live as if you were to die tomorrow. Learn as if you were to live forever." I knew Carol Margaret would throw a Gandhi-ism quote in there somewhere. "It's my time to be brave." Idina Menzel's song is our happy dance in the kitchen as we celebrate our soup of the day.

Bravery

One thing I recognize, with reluctant resignation, is that the only certainty of life in a physical body while living in this world is uncertainty. I am not in control of anything, with the occasional exception; perhaps, of my thoughts, their resulting feelings, intentions, and vision for my life, and my, consequential to those thoughts, responses or actions. The interesting problem with the assumption of control, is, that because my thoughts are always changing, I must learn with absolute consistency to monitor my thoughts so that they become congruent with my desired feelings, clear intentions, expansive vision, and responsible actions. Without consistent practice and awareness, I create room for the presence of chaos, incongruence, dis-ease, imbalance—a self-actualized behemoth wreaking havoc for my world and my every experience in it. In response to all of the behemoths our world has collectively created, I get to gather the courage to conquer my own beast before I can point fingers at any other thinking, acting, co-creating being on this planet. ("All of us," states Maggie in her aspiration of our oneness.)

This chapter addresses my intense desire to be brave when I feel unaware, uncertain, unclear … ("For brevity's sake, just call those feelings 'the uns.'" Carol Margaret is exasperated with my wordiness.) My desires are to be intentional and responsible; to be the change I wish to see in the world; to be the love, the peace, the good; and to delight in my ownership and sharing of a good/love/God vision, committing to bring it to every being everywhere. Hilda was my greatest teacher in the *bravery* department. Thank you, Hilda.

In the first daze of Hilda, I ran a very fast-paced race of a life. Every movement was hurry, go, do; worry, run, get there; and succeed, spend, assess, compare, measure, never stop until collapse was the only option. Interesting that a slow-moving elephant enters my world and my whole mode of operating is squashed by circumstance. Initially I simply ignored her, accelerating into a "go away until I can't anymore" mode. ("Kind of dumped her in your dark and unresolved dilemma stack?" Carol Margaret sorts everything somewhere.) I never took valor out of my trunk, suitcase, pocket, or purse. Bravery isn't necessary when I ignore an issue, and for the first daze with Hilda, I had no wrestling sessions with her. She wasn't my benison or my behemoth—she was just this irritating creature I chose to ignore, with whom I could coexist and feed only when absolutely necessary, and if I went fast enough, that wouldn't be very often because I'd forget about her. No call for true grit, only occasional bravado.

As we aged together, my nonacceptance of her was contributing to roadblocks for the way I wanted my healing to happen and my life to unfold. I needed to stop pretending she wasn't there, and learn to address her as I would a pivotal exam or a tournament tennis game. That required me to slow down enough to pay attention, which was the first requirement in the bracing for bravery game. I learned about Hilda, observed her, and noticed how she affected and attached herself to me. I learned about me and what responsibilities and possibilities I could bring to what I imagined as a game-like adventure, a.k.a., my life. "Let the games begin ..." Carol Margaret is her quotable self, as always.

When Hilda disappeared for a while, I thought my due diligence, responsibility for living the questions into discovery, prayer, visioning, learning, and loving ("and God," Maggie insists) were the causal agents of dismissal. However, when she returned to me after our four-year happy dance, I learned that bravery requires getting up every time I fall down, and never assuming that I'm fall-proof or immune from anxiety or any of the "uns." ("Like a saint," Maggie reiterates.) It's always time to brace for bravery. ("Never take your well-being for granted!" Carol Margaret shakes her finger at me.)

When dearly loved family members or friends were stressed, struggling, ill or dying, bravery looked different than it did when I experienced less eventful, almost peaceful daze without these plentiful aspects of dis-ease and imbalance. The downs of life require grit, spunk, and spirit—all aspects of bravery that are necessary to be and do whatever I must in service for caring, solving, resolving, reconciling, and embracing whatever role I assume in all of my relationships with or without Hilda. I have noticed, upon reflection, that many behemoths and benisons procreated beneath my roof during those years with Hilda—almost like a two-headed buffalo coin. Carol Margaret wants to bet me a nickel that, in reality, benisons and behemoths could not possibly produce such a valuable mistake of coinage. "Humph ..." I ponder.

Mastering circumstance (be Gin) requires different tools from my tool kit depending on the kind of bravery warranted and appropriate for each adventure of creative, full living I endeavor to pour into my soup. If I perceive all of life as blessing and seek to discover the good, the love ("the Center," Maggie says, coming up with a new one for the G-word.), is that choice of perception brave or naïve? Who decides? ("There's no right, wrong, or bad, and you're the only one in charge of yourself." Carol Margaret recites previous note reminders from the corner on her laptop.) Maggie reminds me that choosing to love, seeking what is good, and putting God at the center of my experience is the ultimate methodology for fearless living. I choose to be brave!

So with our chosen methodical approach to masterful courage, we embarked on our new manner of experiencing Hilda and all of her accessories, accompaniments, and activities with renewed zest and opportunity to persevere, endure, outlast, and contain any assault to our chosen bravery operation. Add in a little hope, a lot of prayer, love and support from friends and family, and our formula was perfected. From that point on, we either ceased to acknowledge fear, or if it emerged as an ingredient for our soup, we found ways to make it a healthful addition to our stock.

Carol Margaret quotes the next lines from C. P. Cavafy's "Ithaka": *"Do not fear the monsters of old … You will not meet them in your travels if your thoughts are exalted and remain high, if authentic passions stir your mind, body, and spirit."*

When backbone and spine were challenging (as during my transplant experience when I curled up under my blanket in so much pain, I stopped thinking, feeling, or being anything less than "no thing"), I told myself, "It always gets better. Good, Love, and God always prevail." Maggie insists that a be attitude of trust is bravery at its finest. Thank you, Maggie. Carol Margaret stands erect with an imaginary sword, like a soldier preparing for battle as she quotes Romans 8:28: "For we know that all things work together for good for those who love God and are called according to God's purpose." Maggie takes away our soldier's sword and suggests a universal approach to holy affirmation: "Love and peace are good all the time. All the time peace and love are good." So it is. We nod in agreement.

As Hilda grew larger and more impactful on my being, I grew more aware of my responsibility to choose bravery as a regular state of being. I did it so often that it became my unconscious "go-to" in my transplant experience. I did not feel afraid because I knew with every fiber of my being that all would be well and that all was good, love, and God. Fear is driven out of my attics, closets, basements, and even the dark places of stuffed storage. Fear is recognized for what it is and transformed into a faint yet distinctive seasoning for the soup I stir with my life.

When Hilda was finally gone, I felt a bubbling of fear I never imagined boiling in my soup pot. I pulled the broth-enriched spoon out of the pot, discerned what was on it, and realized that what I thought was fear was only enough room for a beginning again, this time minus an elephant. Carol Margaret, always one to finish what she starts, continues with the next lines from "Ithaka": *"You will not encounter fearful monsters if you do not carry them within your soul, if your soul does not set them up in front of you."*

I can choose to be brave, to seek good, to choose love, and to know God. "And all is well, no matter what!" Maggie asserts gratefully. I also remember that every beginning begins again and again and again. Choice and change are the constants. Bravery, as I've learned to experience it, only enhances the abundance of good gifts I celebrate with gratitude for Hilda. Thank you, good gifts! "And thank you, 'Ithaka,'" we recite in unison.

CHAPTER 15

Good-Bye

The conclusion of an adventure (a.k.a., making room for a new beginning again) includes taking stock of what has been and bringing that "once upon a time" to flavor a now-unfolding beginning into a new and unique story adventure. All adventuring can be good, and many of my experiences have been graceful and grateful beginnings into my be-coming who I truly am. ("Another be word!" Maggie claps her hands with delight.) I keep learning how I can create a life congruent with my intentions for an always opening heart, expanding mind, and healthy body (a.k.a., caregiving for the temple of the spirited soul inhabiting the person of Carol Margaret Hohlfelder Roth). Life in a body is never easy, and although there comes a passage in all of our lives when we take leave of the temples housing our spirits and return to source ("Another beginning, again," Maggie suggests in her passionate positivity.), we get to relish our lives while we're here and make of them what we inspire to create.

When I said good-bye to Hilda (after I eventually realized she had departed from all the hiding places surrounding the presence and possibility that was Carol Margaret Hohlfelder Roth), it was a reflective, prayerful time for me. A "bye" in sports denotes a phantom opponent or a "pass" into the next round without having to play or defeat an existing opponent. ("An advancement, if you will." Carol Margaret likes further edification of all definitives.) My time with Hilda was not a "bye" in my life. Although many suggest cancer is a battle to wage against a foe, Hilda was not my opponent, phantom or otherwise. I wasn't given an advancement or preferential gift for the mysterious creation or disappearance of this elephant. My record was not competitively better or worse than any other animal owners who died with their animals or those who took their leave of them and went on to climb Mt. Everest. Life can't be measured or qualified by competing or comparing performance or experience.

As Carol Margaret's notes remind me, there are no wrong, right, win, and lose conversations that bring healing in union with every other awareness. "Only learning, loving, and God do that," Maggie ardently posits. Healing itself is a mystery, a magical labyrinth we traverse until we reach the center, whatever that is for each of us. We are each individual representations of the good, loving source that made us, and to that source, I believe, we will return. We are part of a holy whole, and in that oneness there are no byes unless there are good-byes for every single piece of the whole. Everyone gets a good good-bye.

So, for me, a "good" good-bye is just an opportunity for another hello—the beginning of another once upon a time, one that includes every once upon a time. That hello is expedited with the miracles brought through grace and gratitude.

Hilda didn't leave me until I accepted her and her presence in my life. I was I, and she was she ... "And that's the way I always heard it should be ..." Maggie was into her rhyming ranting again. Hilda didn't leave me without an abundance of support, service, and love from a lot of people: Donor, doctors, family, friends, pets, strangers, unknown angels ... The list is an infinite number of generous, loving, and amazing souls who cared for me. "Blessings flowering like grace ..." Maggie reminisces.

If I truly desire for who I am to be in congruence with who God is for me, I get to choose to love and accept all creation, to look for good and care for that good—to accept Hilda, to consider my life graced by her presence, and to be grateful for the years we spent together. Getting through an enormous period of painful growth for me was the gift of healing. She was gone, I was great ("And full of it," Carol Margaret mumbles.), and that's when I knew Hilda contributed to the grace and gratitude of my life.

"And it was a graceful and good good-bye!" Maggie exclaims as we feel awed and grateful with her honoring description of Hilda's leave-taking.

Words sometimes can't express our thoughts, emotions, and feelings. We can wave, hug, kick, and scream good-bye. We can bow, Namaste, scowl, slam doors, cry, laugh, wince, turn around to never look back, or gaze wistfully at a retreating figure with longing and loss. A "good-bye" can contain all the emotions, feelings, and thoughts beyond the words. Carol Margaret remembers that music expresses similarly so she immediately consults her extensive collection of good--bye songs for our happy dance of the day. Maggie randomly picks Night Ranger: "Good-Bye." As we happy dance, we celebrate all the practice and ease we're experiencing in the letting go game of life. "For now, at least." Carol Margaret always wants to own the last word and be truly right about it. Maggie encourages me to let go of my eye-rolling remonstrance in response to Carol Margaret's need to be in control and above judgment.

When I think about how Hilda's good-bye graced my life, it seems almost like a benefaction, a blessing, and a benediction. I find myself especially gratified by her graceful departure from my person. My "so what, now what?" has evolved into, "What can I create with this incredible gift of life I've been graced through Hilda's disappearance?" This book has been part of my attempt to share my story, my soup recipe, my happy dance, and my vision for good, love, and God. I like to think that when we are dazed or down, all is good, and that everything always gets better, no matter what. I've learned that humility, vulnerability, courage, waiting, watching, wondering, caring, and enduring allow people to be lifted in flight through the dim places of life. I've learned that when letting go isn't cutting the edges, I can surrender to a higher power, trusting and accepting grace. When I choose faith, life begins to flow into ease. Hope and prayer are powerful aids in the healing into wholeness department. Love can dissipate any fear *all* of the time. Gratitude *always* encourages heart-centered expression. I've learned that what I desire more than anything I've ever wanted is for peace and love to be intended by all of creation so that together we give from our best selves to desire, create, and delight in joy and freedom for every living being. So, if my idea of God isn't the same as yours, dear reader, it's more than okay. I say "good," "love," "God." Perhaps all of us can find some possibility source to "divine," and in that shared divining, we can stir the soup to feed the world, tie blankets to warm all souls, and write stories that restore our oneness, invigorating the wholeness we already are.

I believe divine blessings are always present. Thank you, vision, intention, learning, and possibility. Thank you, Hilda. Thank you, reader. To this adventure: a good good-bye with a grateful and welcome hello to every beginning again.

—Carol Margaret Hohlfelder Roth

Acknowledgments, also known as TGIF: today gratitude is first!

My gratitude extends to everyone who contributed blood, platelets, plasma, time, care, attention, and compassion to me.

To all the doctors, nurses, hospital, and office staff who cared for me before, during, and after Hilda: thank you.

Fabulous friends and kind neighbors, I feel lucky and blessed by your being with me through all the highs and lows.

Family, those souls, as Maggie describes them, "who are gifted to help us learn how to love," for these precious people traveling life with me ... I love you, and thank you for everything!

The world's greatest editor, my favorite writer and Younger Son (a.k.a., Andrew Roth): thank you!

I feel especially thankful for the following contributors to *Hilda*:

My donor (a.k.a., Susan Austin), we're bonded forever, and it's entirely beyond words.

Super Sister (a.k.a., Susan Marie Hohlfelder Ferreri), you are *the* best sister and girlfriend ever.

Number One Husband (a.k.a., Gerry Roth), beloved life partner, best friend, and favorite coadventurer, always I've loved you, and I always will.

Possibility (a.k.a., good, love, God), for providing healing miracles and radical grace, transforming my life into adventurous becoming, I can't begin to fully express my reverent thanksgiving.

And … finally, thank you to Hilda for coaching me into the wholeness I am.

NOTES

Constantine Peter Cavafy (1863–1933) "Ithaka."

Written in 1911, Cavafy's poem's theme is based on the idea that the journey of life is to be enjoyed as a soul's journey through experience to itself/Ithaka/Ithaca. When a soul knows itself, goals and riches are no longer important. Joy is found in valuing the gifts of the journey.

Songs and other writings mentioned in this book include the following:

Anne Lamott, *Help! Thanks! Wow!*

Wayne Dyer, *There's a Spiritual Solution to Every Problem*

Byron Katie, *The Work*

Julian of Norwich (1342–1416), *Revelations*

Paraphrase of Mother Teresa (1910–1997)

Paraphrase of Mahatma Gandhi (1869–1948)

Mutation of "The Wise Old Owl" (unknown author)

Thornton Wilder, Playwright, "Our Town"

Simon and Garfunkel, "Bridge over Troubled Water"

Idina Menzel and Glen Ballard, "Brave"

Charles Strouse (from the musical *Annie*), "Tomorrow"

John Lennon, "Imagine"

Stephen Schwartz (from the musical *Godspell*), "All Good Gifts"

Melissa Etheridge, "A Little Bit of Me"

Night Ranger, "Good-Bye"

Scripture quoted from Revised Standard Version Bible.

ABOUT THE AUTHOR

Carol Roth lives in Carmel, Indiana with her husband of thirty five years. She ardently walks her walk, celebrating any cause that promotes and encourages her life vision for a world where peace and love are intended by and for all creation…except, when she doesn't. Carol is a lifelong learner, lover, forgiver, and beginner again, and an avid writer about all of it (whatever "it" is).